116707

S0-ATO-649

DATE DUE

FEB 1 1 1985	MAY 0 2 1995	
FEB 2 2 1993		
MAR 1 0 1985	APR 1 6 1996	
FEB 1 0 1986	MAY 2 1 1997	
MAY 1 9 1986 MAY MAY 0 1 1997		
FEB 2 3 1987 MAY 1 2 1998		
OCT 2 1989 DEC 1 2 1999		
OCT 2 3 1989		
NOV 2 0 1989		
MAY 2 8 1991		

GAYLORD 234   PRINTED IN U. S. A.

the world that perished

College Library
Glendale Blvd.
Los Angeles, Calif. 90026

.M

the world that perished

john c. whitcomb, jr.

baker book house   grand rapids, michigan

ISBN: 0-8010-9537-9
Copyright © 1973 by Baker Book House Company
Library of Congress Catalog Card Number: 73-84109

First printing, July 1973
Second printing, November 1973

Picture credits

American Museum of Natural History: 29 (top), 79, and 91

George F. Howe: 134

H. Armstrong Roberts: 21, 25, 29 (bottom), 37, 41, 55, 70, 75, 82, 83, 86-87, 101, 109 and 125

Sigurdur Thorarinsson: 143

U.S. National Park Service: 115 (2)

Norma Whitcomb: cover art

Printed in the United States of America

222.11
V581w

LIFE Pacific College
Alumni Library
1100 West Covina Blvd.
San Dimas, CA 91773

To Dr. Donald B. Fullerton
Veteran missionary to India
Missionary to college students since 1931
God's missionary to me on the Princeton campus in 1942

17397

acknowledgments

The author hereby expresses his deep appreciation to the following individuals who have made important contributions to the preparation and production of this book.

Dr. Henry M. Morris, co-author of *The Genesis Flood,* has read the manuscript in its initial form and has written the Foreword.

Three of my faithful colleagues on the faculty of Grace Theological Seminary have read the manuscript and have made numerous valuable suggestions for improving the argumentation and style: *Dr. John J. Davis,* Associate Professor of Old Testament and Hebrew; *Dr. Charles R. Smith,* Associate Professor of Christian Theology and Greek; and *Mr. Robert Ibach, Jr.,* Library Assistant for the Seminary and Teaching Assistant in Old Testament and Archaeology. Mr. Ibach also prepared the Bibliography.

Mr. Cornelius Zylstra and *Mr. Gordon DeYoung* of Baker Book House and *Rev. Charles Turner* of the Brethren Missionary Herald Company have gone beyond their normal bounds of responsibility in planning and producing this work and its companion study, *The Early Earth.*

My beloved wife, Norma, in the midst of many responsibilities of her own, provided the consistent encouragement that I believe to have been God's appointed means for launching and completing this project of many months. The cover painting is her personal contribution.

foreword

We have been living in an age of deep skepticism. A century of evolutionary philosophy, with its seeds of naturalism and atheism, has yielded the bitter fruits of revolution, nonmoralism, and despair.

Nevertheless, even in such an age as this, God has "left not himself without witness, in that he did good and gave you rain from heaven, rains and fruitful seasons, filling your hearts with food and gladness" (Acts 14:17).

There is also another silent, yet eloquent, witness in the very rocks of the earth's crust. In every nation, in the land beneath our feet, and in the hills and valleys through which we travel reposes a vast cemetery. Therein lie the bones and shells, the teeth and trails of innumerable animals, along with the compressed and carbonized remains of immense forests that once filled a beautiful world. Here and there, scattered widely throughout the rocks, can be found artifacts or other fossil evidences even of the human life of long ago.

Modern speculation has managed to distort the testimony of this sedimentary graveyard into a fictional record of slow evolutionary development over a billion years of imaginary earth history. This strange notion has indeed today become accepted and taught as scientific fact in most of our educational institutions all around the world.

Fossils, however, speak of death—not development! Their witness is one of extinction—not evolution. The God who created all things is a God of both power and mercy. He need not and would not have used the principles of suffering and death (especially the massive and violent death implicit in this fossil witness) as implements of creation.

Fossils speak of death, and death speaks of sin and judgment, not of creation and development. When correctly interpreted, whether theologically or scientifically, this world-wide witness in the very earth itself testifies of a sovereign Creator who controls and judges His creation. Rather than evolutionary progress over many ages, these stones cry out concerning a judicial termination of *one* age.

This brief but incisive book by John Whitcomb expounds with no uncertain sound the Biblical record of that great hydrodynamic convulsion with which God judged the wickedness of the antediluvian world. Whatever geological problems may be suggested, there can no longer be *any* question that, if the word of God be true, the Genesis Flood was a world-covering, cataclysmic judgment imposed by the strong hand of God.

God has thus not left Himself in these last days without human witnesses, either. One of the most effective of those who witness for God's truth today is the author of this book. His testimony, as seminary professor, as Bible conference teacher, as a knowledgeable and cogent writer, and as a gracious Christian gentleman, has been a blessing to many thousands during the past two decades. It is a high privilege to recommend, with real enthusiasm, this outstanding new book by John C. Whitcomb, a man who, like Apollos, is "mighty in the scriptures" and "fervent in the spirit" (Acts 18:24, 25) as well as a beloved colleague and friend in Christ.

San Diego   Henry M. Morris
February, 1973

preface

"The world that then was, being overflowed with water, perished" (II Peter 3:6). With these words, the apostle Peter establishes beyond any reasonable doubt the validity of what has come to be known as "Biblical catastrophism" or "Flood geology." Anticipating the day when men would deny the possibility of God's direct intervention in global judgment at the end of history ("Where is the promise of His coming?"), Peter uses the analogy of the Great Flood of Noah's day to dispel forever the validity of the pseudo-scientific philosophy of total uniformitarianism.

It is the purpose of this study to restate in a more popular form the basic Biblical and scientific evidences for that Flood, as set forth originally in *The Genesis Flood* (co-authored with Dr. Henry M. Morris in 1961), and to bring up to date the great controversy which that and similar works have stirred up. The author has also attempted to analyze and to answer briefly the published objections that have been leveled against *The Genesis Flood* in the past twelve years.

The author is grateful to God for the remarkable response accorded by the Christian public to the first study of this series (*The Early Earth,* 1972), and trusts that He may be pleased, in His good providence, to use this small volume in a similar way to create a wider interest in the study of His infallible Word during these last days before His coming.

contents

1
God destroyed the world
..supernaturally

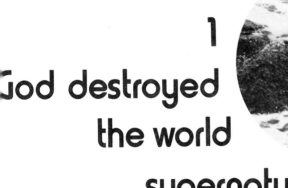

THE HISTORICITY OF persons and events connected with the great Flood described in the early chapters of Genesis is confirmed in six New Testament passages.[1] In at least *five* of these six passages, *the supernatural origin of the Deluge is either stated or implied.* In Matthew 24:37-42 and in Luke 17:26-27, the Lord Jesus Christ compared the Flood (in which one righteous family was left to repopulate the world while all wicked men were taken away) with the Second Coming, when some will be left and others will be taken in judgment. In Hebrews 11:7 we are told that Noah was "warned of God of things not seen as yet," clearly implying the supernatural origin and character of the Deluge. In II Peter 2:4-5 we read that "God . . . brought a flood upon the world of the ungodly." Likewise, according to II Peter 3:5-6, it was "by the word of God" that "the world that then was, being overflowed with water, perished," even as "the heavens that now are, and the earth, *by the same word* have been stored up for fire, being reserved against the day of judgment and destruction of ungodly men" (vs. 7).[2]

Even as Christians have frequently been guilty of distorting the Biblical account of creation by reading into it the concept of mere natural processes acting through vast periods of time,[3] so also has the Biblical record of the great Flood suffered severely at the hands of uniformitarian interpreters in our day.

Geologists are certainly correct when they insist that a world-wide, mountain-covering Flood could not occur today on the basis of observable geologic processes, and the present balance of suboceanic and continental masses. We agree that there is no *known* force or combination of forces in the crust of the earth sufficiently powerful to elevate all the ocean floors and to submerge all the continents and then reverse the process within one year!

But when these same geologists (as well as those theologians who are deeply influenced by currently popular geological theories) assert dogmatically that the Book of Genesis is wrong when it tells us of this kind of global catastrophe in the days of Noah, are they not underestimating the God

---

1. Matthew 24:37-39; Luke 17:26-27; Hebrews 11:7; I Peter 3:20; II Peter 2:5, and II Peter 3:5-7.
2. All quotations of Scripture, unless otherwise noted, are taken from the American Standard Version, 1901.
3. See J. C. Whitcomb, Jr., *The Early Earth* (Grand Rapids: Baker Book House, 1972), pp. 24-29.

of creation, miracle, and judgment? In the words of our Lord Jesus Christ, "Ye do err, not knowing the scriptures, nor the power of God" (Matt. 22:29).

In the first place, we dare not ignore the statements of Scripture concerning *the supernatural forces* which God employed in launching the great Flood so that it was not a mere chance combination of natural and presently observable processes. In fact, Scripture presents the Flood as a unique, once-for-all, never-to-be-repeated event of earth history, comparable in magnitude and significance only to the final judgment of the world (Gen. 8:21-9:17; Matt. 24:37-42; and II Peter 3:5-7).

Second, and even more serious, such scientists and theologians "wilfully forget" (II Peter 3:5) that God is not only living and personal, but is completely capable of accomplishing exactly the kinds of miracles attested to in His Word. In fact, the Bible is emphatically clear that no one can be a true Christian apart from an acceptance of such stupendous miracles as the bodily resurrection of Jesus Christ from the grave on the third day following His crucifixion (Rom. 10:9; I Cor. 15:1-10).

Advocates of the local Flood concept have always found it convenient, of course, to question the validity of the appeal to miracles that *must* characterize any serious attempt to cope with the Biblical doctrine of the Flood. Bernard Ramm is a theologian who believes in Biblical miracles but is nevertheless quite emphatic in insisting that "if one wishes to retain a universal flood, it must be understood that a series of stupendous miracles are [sic] required. Further, one cannot beg off with pious statements that God can do anything. ... There is no question what Omnipotence can do, but *the simplicity of the Flood record* prohibits the endless supplying of miracles to make a universal flood feasible."[4]

In considering this objection, our attention is focused, in the first place, on the statement that "the simplicity of the flood record" prohibits the kind of supernaturalism that a universal Flood would call for. Dr. Ramm does not go on to tell us the nature of this supposed "simplicity," and this is unfortunate, for it is apparent that this serves as his interpretive key for the entire Flood narrative of Genesis.

---

4. Bernard Ramm, *The Christian View of Science and Scripture* (Grand Rapids: Wm. B. Eerdmans Pub. Co., 1954), pp. 243-47. Italics added. As will be shown below (pp. 19-42), the Biblical concept of the Flood does not involve an "endless supplying of miracles."

In the light of this, one cannot help but ask whether the Biblical description of *any* miracle is not characterized by a certain "simplicity." How would Dr. Ramm distinguish between "Genesis miracles" and, say, "Daniel miracles" or "Matthew miracles"?

In the second place, the present writer is not aware of the necessity of appealing to "an endless supplying of miracles to make a universal Flood feasible." As we shall seek to demonstrate in Chapter 3, some very important aspects of the Flood involved an outworking of natural laws and processes through the *providence* (as contrasted with the supernatural intervention) of God.

The most serious problem with Dr. Ramm's position, however, is its failure to come to terms with the Biblical testimony to *the basically supernatural framework of the Genesis Flood*. It is not a question of appealing desperately to the "sheer omnipotence of God" to prop up an unscriptural theory of catastrophism, but rather of taking into account the clear statements of the Biblical text concerning the causes and effects of the Flood. A careful analysis of the relevant exegetical data reveals at least six areas in which supernaturalism is clearly demanded in the doctrine of the Flood: (1) the divinely-revealed design of the Ark; (2) the gathering and care of the animals; (3) the uplift of oceanic waters from beneath; (4) the release of waters from above; (5) the formation of our present ocean basins; and (6) the formation of our present continents and mountain ranges. Each of these supernatural aspects of the Flood constitutes a radical break with the naturalistic presuppositions of modern scientism and for this reason deserves our careful consideration.

The Design of the Ark

One hundred and twenty years before the Flood came, God revealed to one human being His purpose to destroy the earth by water and instructed him to make preparation for this judgment by building an ark that would be the instrument for saving not only his family but also the seed of of all air-breathing creatures in the world. This structure was significant not only for its spatial dimensions and proportions, as we shall see, but also in its time dimension; for the hundred years of its construction provided a visible demonstration of God's unwillingness that any man should perish and served as an open invitation to salvation from impending doom. As the apostle Peter expressed it, "the patience of

NOAH'S ARK COMPARED TO MODERN SHIPS

Noah's Ark was the largest sea-going vessel ever built, until the late nineteenth century when giant metal ships were first constructed. The Ark was approximately 450 feet by 75 feet; but as late as 1858 "the largest vessel of her type in the world was the P & O liner *Himalaya,* 240 feet by 35 feet . . . ." In that year, Isambard K. Brunel produced "the *Great Eastern*, 692 feet by 83 feet by 30 feet of approximately 19,000 tons . . . five times the tonnage of any ship then afloat. So vast was Brunel's leap that even forty years later in an age of fierce competition the largest liners being built were still smaller than the *Great Eastern*. . . . The Babylonian account which speaks of the Ark as a cube betrays complete ignorance. Such a vessel would spin slowly around. But the Biblical ratios leave nothing to be desired. These ratios are important from the point of view of stability, of pitching and of rolling. The ratio of length to breadth, 300 to 50, is 6 to 1. Taking the mean of six present-day ships of approximately the same size, selected from six different shipping lines, we obtain, as an example, a ratio of 8.1 to 1. The giant liner *Queen Elizabeth* has a ratio 8.6 to 1 while the *Canberra* has 8.2 to 1. But these vessels were designed for speed; the Ark was not. Some of the giant tankers have ratios around 7 to 1. Still more interesting are the figures for the *Great Britain*, designed by I. K. Brunel in 1844. Her dimensions were 322 feet by 51 feet by 32½ feet, so that the ratios are almost exactly those of the Ark. Brunel had the accumulated knowledge of generations of shipbuilders to draw upon. The Ark was the first of its kind!" (Frederick A. Filby, *The Flood Reconsidered*, p. 93).

God kept waiting in the days of Noah, during the construction of the ark" (I Peter 3:20, NASB).

The spatial dimensions of the Ark constitute a remarkable testimony to the internal consistency and objective rationality of the Biblical Flood account. Whereas the Babylonian flood account abounds in absurdities and speaks of the Ark as a perfect cube 120 cubits in each direction and with nine decks,[5] the God-revealed dimensions recorded in Genesis are both reasonable and appropriate in their proportions and magnitude in the light of the intended purpose of the Ark. With regard to its proportions, "a model was made by Peter Jansen of Holland, and Danish barges called *Fleuten* were modeled after the Ark. These models proved that the Ark had a greater capacity than curved or shaped vessels. They were very seaworthy and almost impossible to capsize."[6]

Henry Morris, in a recent study of the stability of the Ark, has concluded that *it would have to be turned completely vertical* before it could be tipped over. "Furthermore," Dr. Morris continues, "its relatively great length (six times its width) would tend to keep it from being subjected to wave forces of equal magnitude through its whole length, since wave fields tend to occur in broken and varying patterns, rather than in a series of long uniform crest-trough sequences, and this would be particularly true in the chaotic hydrodynamic phenomena of the Flood. The Ark would, in fact, tend to be lined up by the spectrum of hydrodynamic forces and currents in such a direction that its long axis would be parallel to the predominant direction of wave and current movement. Thus it would act as a semi-streamlined body, and the net drag forces would usually be minimal. In every way, therefore, the Ark as designed was highly stable, admirably suited for its purpose of riding out the storms of the year of the great Flood."[7] As a flat-bottomed barge, not designed to move through the water, but simply to float, it had one-third more carrying capacity than a ship with sloping sides of similar dimensions.[8]

Even more important, the dimensions of the Ark were

5. E. A. Speiser, trans., "The Epic of Gilgamesh," in *Ancient Near Eastern Texts Relating to the Old Testament,* 3rd ed.; edited by James B. Pritchard (Princeton: Princeton University Press, 1969), p. 93.
6. Bernard Ramm, *The Christian View,* p. 230.
7. Henry M. Morris, "The Ark of Noah," *Creation Research Society Quarterly* (Sept., 1971), pp. 142-44.
8. Cf. Alexander Heidel, *The Gilgamesh Epic and Old Testament Parallels* (2nd ed., Chicago: University of Chicago Press, 1949), p. 246.

sufficiently great to accomplish its intended purpose of saving alive the thousands of kinds of air-breathing creatures that could not otherwise survive a year-long Flood. Assuming the length of the cubit to have been at least 17.5 inches, the available floor space of this three-decked barge was over 95,000 square feet, and its total volume was 1,396,000 cubic feet.[9]

Such figures are difficult to picture without comparisons. For the sake of realism, imagine waiting at a railroad crossing while ten freight trains, each pulling 52 boxcars, move slowly by, one after another. That is how much space was available in the Ark, for its capacity was equivalent to 520 modern railroad stock cars. A barge of such gigantic size, with its thousands of built-in compartments (Gen. 6:14) would have been sufficiently large to carry two of every *species* of air-breathing animal in the world today (and doubtless the tendency toward taxonomic splitting has produced more "species" than can be justified in terms of Genesis "kinds") on only half of its available deck space.[10] The remaining space would have been occupied by Noah's family, five additional representatives of each of the comparatively few kinds of animals acceptable for sacrifice, two each of the kinds that have become extinct since the Flood, and food for them all (Gen. 6:21).

In the light of these statistics, two observations seem appropriate. First, the supernatural revelation granted to Noah concerning the Ark, a century before the Flood, serves to emphasize the fact that the Flood was not a mere natural/ providential event in earth history, which was at a later time interpreted poetically as a "miracle" of judgment. Instead, the hundred-year advance warning and detailed preparations by Noah put the Flood into the category of an eschatological, apocalyptic event, as far as the antediluvian world was concerned.

In the second place, the size and proportions of the Ark constitute a strong apologetic for the divine inspiration of the

9. Dr. Millard Erickson, Professor of Theology at Bethel Theological Seminary, St. Paul, Minnesota, made a serious blunder of calculation at this point: "Since the fundamentalist usually held that the flood in Genesis covered the entire earth, there were also some problems in getting at least two specimens of all the present animal species (except fish and amphibians) into a ship with less than 35,000 square feet of floor space." *The New Evangelical Theology* (Westwood, N.J.: Fleming H. Revell Co., 1968), p. 160.

10. Cf. Whitcomb and Morris, *The Genesis Flood* (Nutley, N.J.: Presbyterian & Reformed Pub. Co., 1961), pp. 65-69.

Book of Genesis, for if Moses had simply invented the story, or had revised some current flood legends, he could not have described the Ark in the way we find it in the Book of Genesis. He could not have known how large such a structure would have to be to fulfill such a purpose, as we now realize in the light of recent discoveries of the vast number of different kinds of air-breathing animals in the world.

The Gathering and Care of the Animals

A second major aspect of the supernaturalism of the Flood pertains to the air-breathing creatures that survived. In the very nature of the case, it would have been quite impossible for Noah and his family to have gathered thirty or forty thousand animals (of half that many kinds) into the Ark, even if they had spent the entire century doing nothing else.

A rather amusing illustration of this fact occurred recently in Italy, a few miles south of Rome, when a film producer attempted to depict the story of the animals and the Ark. Much time and effort were expended in training a few zoo animals to walk two by two up a ramp into a model of the Ark. When the time came for the filming, however, "a water buffalo charged up the gangway, crashed through the ark and headed for Rome at full snort." After that, as the report continued, "the jungle's rougher embarkees were filmed behind glass."[11] All of which simply confirms the obviously supernatural factors at work in this phase of the Flood event.

But some evangelical scientists claim that only domesticated animals were taken into the Ark, and thus it would not have been an impossible task for Noah and his family. A Canadian scientist, Arthur Custance, writes: "It is almost certain that domesticated animals could not have migrated alone. . . . For this reason, if for no other, some animals at least would have to be taken on board . . . but these were probably of the domesticated varieties."[12]

George Cansdale, a British zoo director and author of *Animals of Bible Lands* (London: Paternoster Press, 1970), agrees that "Noah's main job was to save the breeding stock of the domesticated animals closely associated with man and largely dependent on him, thus allowing a quick start in oc-

---

11. Michael A. Vaccaro, "A Literal View of the Bible in Huston's New Movie: NOAH," *Look Magazine,* July 27, 1965, p. 25.
12. Arthur C. Custance, *The Extent of the Flood: Doorway Papers #41* (Brockville, Ontario: By the Author, Box 291, 1958), p. 9.

KANGAROOS AND NOAH'S ARK

Question: How could kangaroos have traveled from Australia to Noah's Ark? *Answer*: They didn't. At least two each of all the kinds of air-breathing animals—including kangaroos—must have lived on the same continent where the Ark was built, so they could come to Noah by divine guidance (Gen. 6:20; 7:9) without having to cross oceans.

Question: How did kangaroos reach Australia from Mount Ararat after the Flood? *Answer*: A great land bridge apparently connected Asia and Australia in the early post-Flood period. During this most intense phase of the "ice age," such vast quantities of water were locked in the polar regions that ocean levels were hundreds of feet lower than they are now. The National Geographic map of the *Pacific Ocean Floor* (October, 1969) clearly shows the shallow continental shelf that extends even now from Indochina almost to Australia.

cupying the ground which had been severely damaged, but not all entirely ruined, by the deluge."[13]

In a more recent work, *The Flood Reconsidered,* F. A. Filby, a British chemist, follows the same line of thought. He maintains that if we eliminate the wild animals from the Ark most of the difficulties disappear;

> The giraffe would have have required a special stall to enable him to stretch his neck—but if Central Africa was not part of the world Noah knew, no problem arises. The mastodon of South America must have made a long journey to reach Sumeria and the giant panda from China would have required a special stock of bamboo shoots for his year's food—but it seems that the Bible does not really require mastodons and giant pandas in the ark. . . . It is far more reasonable to suppose that Noah collected—maybe tamed—oxen, sheep, goats, horses, asses, camels, relatives of the deer, animals of the cat, dog, beaver, fox, pig, mole, rat and rabbit tribes, and many birds. . . . Noah probably found it necessary to include only a small number of the world's carnivores.[14]

But where does the Book of Genesis suggest that Noah was to take only domesticated animals into the Ark? The purpose of the Flood was to destroy "both man, and beast, and creeping things, and birds of the heavens" (6:7), and "to destroy all flesh, wherein is the breath of life, from under heaven" (6:17; cf. 6:12-13, 19-21; 7:2-4, 8, 14-16; 8:1, 17-19; 9:8-17). These are exactly the same terms used in the first chapter of Genesis to describe the various kinds of land animals which God created. If only domesticated animals were to be taken into the Ark, are we to assume that only domesticated animals were created by God in the first chapter of Genesis? The fact of the matter is that no clearer terms could have been employed by the author than those which he did employ to express the idea of *the totality of air-breathing animals in the world.* Once this point is conceded, all controversy as to the geographical extent of the Deluge must end; for no one would care to maintain that all land animals were confined to the Mesopotamian Valley in the days of Noah!

---

13. George S. Cansdale, "A Universal Flood: Some Practical Difficulties," *Faith and Thought* (Journal of the Victoria Institute), Vol. 98, Nos. 2 and 3, 1970, p. 66.
14. Frederick A. Filby, *The Flood Reconsidered* (Grand Rapids: Zondervan Pub. House, 1971), pp. 85, 86.

At this point we must pause to ask ourselves a very important question. If we insist on making the gathering of the animals entirely reasonable to the unregenerate mind by eliminating all the supernatural elements, *have we not also succeeded in making the Biblical account completely unreasonable?* Note, for example, this explanation by Dr. Filby: "In cases of impending danger, animals, particularly younger ones, look for someone to protect them. We can well believe that with a raging storm outside, and warmth, food, comfort and safety within the Ark the attitude of most of the animals to Noah (even apart from any Divine overruling which could certainly have been exercised) would have been that of pets looking to their owners for protection and friendship."[15] But would all of these animals have suddenly become docile pets just because of a storm? Furthermore, the text of Genesis informs us that the "storm" did not begin until after all the animals were in the Ark! As we ponder such "harmonizations" between science and Scripture, we find ourselves concurring with the judgment of Andrew D. White that "each mixes up more or less of science with more or less of Scripture, and produces a result more or less absurd."[16]

In his popular work *The Biblical Flood and the Ice Epoch,* Donald Patten also attempts to explain the gathering of the animals without appealing to God's miraculous intervention. But his explanation at the same time practically shifts us into the realm of absurdities. After giving several examples of the abnormal behavior of animals just prior to natural catastrophes, he states: "Animals spoken of in the Genesis account, domestic and probably wild ones as well, entered the Ark seven days prior to the Flood—seven days before the rain commenced and surging waters from the oceans began to heave. *Apparently there were significant forewarnings, microvibrations or minute foreshocks of the coming catastrophe, seismic in nature.*"[17]

---

15. Filby, *The Flood Reconsidered,* p. 86.
16. Andrew D. White, *A History of the Warfare of Science with Theology in Christendom* (New York: George Braziller, reprinted 1955), p. 234.
17. Donald W. Patten, *The Biblical Flood and the Ice Epoch* (Seattle: Pacific Meridian Pub. Co., 1966), p. 64. Italics added. Although mildly critical of Immanuel Velikovsky's views (pp. 138, 208), he nevertheless follows the same basic approach of seeking to explain many of the great miraculous events recorded in Scripture (e.g., the Exodus from Egypt, p. 181) in terms of purely chance astral catastrophism. Patten believes in an original creation (p. 266) but

INDONESIAN AND AMERICAN "DINOSAURS"

Evolutionary scientists believe that dinosaurs became extinct many millions of years before men appeared on earth. But the Bible indicates that men and dinosaurs have lived contemporaneously. For example, Romans 5:12 and 8:20-22 indicate that *there was no death in the animal kingdom until Adam sinned.* Thus, the death and fossilization of dinosaurs must have occurred *after the Edenic Curse of Genesis 3.* That such dinosaurs as the *brontosaurus* lived in some Near Eastern river valleys as late as 2,000 B.C. is indicated in Job 40:15-19 ("Behold now, behemoth . . . he eateth grass as an ox. . . . He moveth his tail like a cedar. . . . He is the chief of the ways of God.") The marginal explanation in the A.S.V. and the N.A.S.B. that this is the hippopotamus is clearly contradicted by the reference to his "tail like a cedar."

Scientific discovery confirms Biblical revelation at this point. Human footprints have been found with the footprints of reptilian dinosaurs (see Whitcomb and Morris, *The Genesis Flood,* pp. 172-76). If we understand "dinosaur" in its original meaning of "terrible lizard," then dinosaurs are not yet extinct! About 1,000 huge *dragon lizards* (top photo) still survive on the small Indonesian island of Komodo (see *National Geographic Magazine,* Dec., 1968, pp. 872-80). Although they are now 99% extinct and seldom exceed 12 feet in length, the *American alligator* (bottom photo) attained lengths of nearly 20 feet as recently as the turn of the century (see *National Geographic Magazine,* Jan., 1967, p. 137). Only about 500 years ago the *aepyornis,* a dinosaur bird over 10 feet tall and weighing half a ton, still lived on the island of Madagascar (see *National Geographic Magazine,* Oct., 1967, p. 493). The time has come for a totally new perspective on dinosaurs!

Now what exactly is Patten asking us to believe here? His theory is that two of all kinds of air-breathing creatures and seven each of the kinds acceptable for sacrifice were impelled toward the Ark by a series of microvibrations in the crust of the earth caused by the planet Mercury as it swept past the earth into its present orbit. Is this the kind of help that the secular, sophisticated mind of the twentieth century needs in order to begin taking the Genesis account seriously? The answer seems obvious.

George Cansdale apparently abandons the storm theory of Filby and the astral visitor theory of Patten and puts the entire burden upon Noah himself. "The men of that early period," Cansdale assures us, "were able to catch, train, and domesticate a range of large, wild . . . and unlikely animals, showing an expertise that has long since been lost."[18] But how does this explanation really come to grips with Genesis 6:20, in which God promises to Noah that "two of every sort shall come to thee, to keep them alive"? Cansdale answers by appealing to the preceding and more general statement of 6:19 ("two of every sort shalt thou bring into the ark") and by ignoring the final and more detailed statements of Genesis 7:9 ("there went in two and two unto Noah into the ark, the male and the female, as God had commanded Noah") and 7:16 ("they that went in, went in male and female of all flesh, as God commanded him: and Jehovah shut him in"). Robert Jamieson admitted that "they must have been prompted by an overruling divine direction, as it is impossible, on any other principle, to account for their going in *pairs.*"[19] Bernard Ramm, who denies the concept of a universal Flood and objects to an "endless supplying of miracles," nevertheless agrees that the animals had to be "prompted by a divine instinct" to go into the Ark.[20]

When all else fails, why not cut the Gordian knot of endless speculation and simply acknowledge that *God, and God alone,* had the power to bring two each of the basic kinds of air-breathing creatures to the Ark, and that Noah's task

also reveals a weak view of the authority of God's Word (p. 216 footnote; 307). For a critical view of his book by Henson, Mulfinger, Reymond, and Williams, see the *Creation Research Society Quarterly,* March, 1968, pp. 129-32. See also Alvin O. Ramsley's review in *Journal of the American Scientific Affiliation* (hereafter referred to as *JASA*), Dec., 1967, pp. 122-23.
18. Cansdale, "A Universal Flood," pp. 65-66.
19. *Jamieson, Fausset, and Brown Commentary* (Grand Rapids: Wm. B. Eerdmans Pub. Co., reprinted 1948), I, 95.
20. Ramm, *The Christian View,* p. 249.

of building the Ark was undoubtedly sufficient to keep him fully occupied? Multitudes who had laughed at Noah's warnings (cf. Heb. 11:7; I Peter 3:20; II Peter 2:5) must have been profoundly impressed and even terrified by this ominous spectacle of tens of thousands of animals coming to the Ark, obviously led by the power of God!

But this is not the end of objections from modern scholars. Even assuming that somehow the animals could have been gathered into the Ark, certain Christian scholars assure us that it would have been an impossible task for Noah and his family to cope with such an enormous assemblage of creatures in a floating barge for a year. In order to ridicule the universal Flood concept, dismal word pictures are drawn of wild animals terrified by the movements of the Ark upon the waters, while the desperate human inmates of this floating menagerie attempted in vain to calm them and to cope with the ever-increasing sanitation problem.[21] Bernard Ramm, for example, feels that "the task of carrying away the manure, and bringing food would completely overtax the few people in the ark."[22]

Such a picture is completely contrary to the clear statements and implications of Scripture. Our God is a God of order, not of confusion (I Cor. 14:33, 40). Having led Noah into this situation by supernatural means, would God's power no longer be available to sustain him (cf. Phil. 1:6; Gal. 3:3)? An analogous situation was faced by the human author of the Book of Genesis many years later when he led his people out of bondage in Egypt by the supernatural help of God, only to face the barren wilderness and the apparently hopeless situation of finding food and water there for millions of people. Did the supernatural provisions of God fail Moses and his people then? Every student of Scripture knows the answer to that question.

Now, if we look closely at Genesis 8:1, we will find an important key to the solution of this apparently unanswerable problem. We are told here that God *"remembered"* Noah and all the animals in the Ark. "When the Old Testament says that *God remembered,* it combines the ideas of faithful love (cf. Jer. 2:2; 31:20) and timely intervention: 'God's remembering always implies his movement towards the object of his memory.' (Cf. Gen. 19:29; Exod. 2:24; Luke

---

21. Cf. Custance, *The Extent of the Flood,* pp. 19-20.
22. Ramm, *The Christian View,* p. 246.

1:54, 55)."[23] But how did God do this in the case of Noah and the animals? We believe that He supernaturally imposed a year-long hibernation or estivation experience, whereby the bodily functions of these animals were reduced to a minimum, and thus removed the burden of their care completely from the hands of Noah and his family.

What Biblical evidence do we find to support this significant concept? *First,* we must assume that God supernaturally controlled the bodily functions of these animals to bring them to the Ark in the first place, overcoming all of their natural instincts during that period of time. All alternative possibilities have been shown to be hopelessly inadequate. *Second,* there could have been no multiplication of animals (not even the rabbits!) during the year of the Flood, for the Ark was built just large enough to carry two of each, and the animals entered the Ark two by two and a year later went out of the Ark two by two. Note that it was not until *after* Noah brought the creatures out of the Ark that God commanded them to "breed abundantly in the earth, and be fruitful, and multiply upon the earth" (8:17). It might be added that even if only domesticated animals were taken on board (as Cansdale, Filby, Custance, and Ramm affirm), it *still* would have been a gigantic if not impossible task for eight people to care for *hundreds* of animals in a floating barge for months!

In the entire matter of gathering the animals to the Ark and caring for them during the year of the Flood, the Book of Genesis is *consistently supernatural* in its presentation. These important facts cannot be properly harmonized with a concept of the Flood that would reduce it to the level of "simplicity" in terms of a series of natural/providential events.

The Uplift of Oceanic Waters

A third supernatural aspect of the Flood was the uplift of oceanic waters through the breaking up of "the fountains of the great deep" (Gen. 7:11). The Bible excludes the possi-

23. Derek Kidner, *Genesis: An Introduction and Commentary* (Chicago: Inter-Varsity Press, 1967), p. 92. See also F. Brown, S. R. Driver, and C. A. Briggs, *A Hebrew and English Lexicon of the Old Testament* (Oxford: At the Clarendon Press, 1968), p. 270. Hannah prayed: "O Jehovah of hosts, if thou wilt ... *remember* me" (I Sam 1:11). In his hour of need, "Samson called unto Jehovah, and said, O Lord Jehovah, *remember* me" (Judges 16:28). The dying thief cried out: "Jesus, *remember* me" (Luke 23:43). In each case, consider the *spectacular* provision God made in response.

bility of a mere fortuitous combination of natural geologic causes here, for we are told that this involved *"all* the fountains of the great deep," and that they were all broken up "on the *same day,"* namely, the seventeenth day of the second month of the six hundredth year of Noah's life.[24] This was indeed a noteworthy day in world history, for in that day God completely upset the delicate balances of the primeval continents and oceans (cf. Isa. 40:12) and initiated a catastrophe so gigantic that the "world [*cosmos*] that then was, being overflowed with water, perished" (II Peter 3:6).

This uplift of ocean basins, accompanied by enormous explosions of suboceanic and subterranean magmas and steam,[25] together with a corresponding sinking of continents, continued for six weeks until the Flood attained its maximum, mountain-covering depth (7:20); and this depth was maintained for another 110 days until the waters had destroyed every living thing on the continents. The uniqueness of this geologic discontinuity in earth history is emphasized in Genesis 8:21-22 ("neither will I again smite any more everything living, as I have done. While the earth remaineth, seedtime and harvest, and cold and heat, and summer and winter, and day and night shall not cease"). Furthermore, the terms of the rainbow covenant in Genesis 9:8-17 and its repetition in Isaiah 54:9 ("I have sworn that the waters of Noah shall no more go over the earth") confirm the supernatural uniqueness of this global catastrophe.

The Release of Waters from Above

Most commentators tend to interpret "the waters which were above the firmament" of Genesis 1:7 simply in terms of rain clouds because of a tacit assumption that present atmospheric conditions have continued, basically unchanged, since creation. However, this concept is in serious conflict

---

24. The hundred year warning given to Noah, the supernatural gathering of the animals, and the chronology of the Flood year make it exceedingly difficult to take seriously the "astral catastrophism" theories of Velikovsky and Patten. Patten feels that unless we can demonstrate *scientifically* how the Flood occurred, "geology may easily hibernate in its present uniformitarian bed for another 100 years" (*The Biblical Flood and the Ice Epoch,* p. 20). But his attempt to explain the Flood as the natural consequence of an astral intrusion which upset the earth's equilibrium ignores clear Biblical statements describing and requiring supernatural works on the part of God. This raises the question as to whether Genesis is being *manipulated* to fit a preconceived theory.

25. Cf. Whitcomb and Morris, *The Genesis Flood,* pp. 122, 127, 387-89.

with the plain statement of Genesis 7:11-12, that "the windows of heaven were opened. And the rain was upon the earth forty days and forty nights." This can refer to nothing less than the collapse of a stupendous transparent vapor canopy that existed only during the antediluvian period, for it required *six weeks* for this water to pour down upon the earth. By contrast, if all the water vapor and clouds in the present atmosphere were precipitated to earth, the rain would last only a few hours and would produce an average depth of less than two inches.[26]

If a vapor canopy of such magnitude existed from the second day of creation week to the time of the Flood, then climatic conditions must have been quite different from those we observe today. In the first place, it is probable that it never rained until the time of the Flood (cf. Hebrews 11:7—"things not seen as yet"), and that throughout the entire antediluvian age "there went up a mist from the earth, and watered the whole face of the ground" (Gen. 2:5-6).[27]

Secondly, there were no great variations in the climate in different parts of the earth because of the greenhouse effect of the vapor canopy.[28] Not until after these waters fell to earth are we told of great winds (8:1), which would imply significant temperature differences between equatorial and polar regions for the first time. In these polar regions, where tropical plants and animals once lived in abundance, huge masses of snow and ice suddenly began to accumulate.

Thus, "the world that then was," as the apostle Peter describes the pre-Flood cosmos, differed profoundly from "the heavens that now are, and the earth" (II Peter 3:7). One of the greatest causes of this difference, we believe, was the supernatural opening of the "windows of heaven,"[29] whereby the waters that were above the atmospheric expanse ("firma-

---

26. Cf. Lincoln Barnett, ed., *The World We Live In* (New York: Time, Inc., 1955), p. 81.
27. Cf. Leupold, *Exposition of Genesis* (Grand Rapids: Baker Book House, 1949), pp. 112-14. For a contrary opinion, cf. R. Laird Harris, "The Mist, The Canopy, and the Rivers of Eden," *Bulletin of the Evangelical Theological Society,* Vol. 11, No. 4 (Fall, 1968), pp. 177-79.
28. Cf. Whitcomb and Morris, *The Genesis Flood,* pp. 253-55. An additional source of Flood waters besides the oceans seems to be implied in II Peter 3:5—"out of water and amidst water."
29. A comparison of II Kings 7:2, Isaiah 24:18, and Malachi 3:10 shows that Jews understood "windows of heaven" to be a figure of speech.

ment")[30] fell to earth in a never-to-be-repeated universal rain to rejoin the earth's oceans for the first time since the second day of creation week. Therefore, miraculous intervention, rather than a mere providential concurrence of natural forces such as are available for geologic activity today, provides once more the essential key for interpreting the dynamics of the Flood and the profound geologic and meteorologic changes that it introduced.

The Formation of Our Present Ocean Basins

Even as the beginning of the Flood year was characterized by supernatural intervention, so also the end of the Flood was brought about by a stupendous miracle of God. Apart from this, the waters would have covered the earth forever, and all terrestrial life would soon have come to an end.

Two passages of Scripture, in widely separated Old Testament books, deal with this particular activity of God. The first, in Genesis 8:2-3, tells us that "the fountains . . . of the deep . . . were stopped . . . and the waters returned from off the earth continually." Since the breaking up of the fountains of the great deep involved the uplift of ocean floors, the stopping of these "fountains" must refer to a reversal of this action, whereby new and much deeper ocean basins were formed to serve as vast reservoirs for the two oceans which were separated from each other by the atmospheric expanse before the Flood (Gen. 1:7). A natural result of this subsidence was that "the waters returned from off the earth continually," permitting continents to emerge from the oceans again, as they had done on the third day of creation.

A second passage that sheds important light upon the termination of the Flood is Psalm 104:6-9. Though it contains several figures of speech, the passage is clearly historical in its reference to the Flood. Note, for example, the statement of verse 6—"the waters stood above the mountains," and that of verse 9—"thou hast set a bound that they may not pass over; That they turn not again to cover the earth." The latter is obviously a reference to the rainbow covenant of

---

30. Genesis 1:6-8. Paul H. Seely ("The Three-Storied Universe," *JASA,* March, 1969, pp. 18-22) denies the reality of the Biblical "firmament" by distorting its meaning. For effective clarifications, see R. Laird Harris and Robert C. Newman, Letters to the Editor, *JASA,* September, 1969, pp. 92-93; and Walter C. Kaiser, Jr., "The Literary Form of Genesis 1-11," in *New Perspectives on the Old Testament,* ed. by J. Barton Payne (Waco, Texas: Word Books, Inc., 1970), pp. 57-58.

THE OCEAN SHORELINE — A PERPETUAL BOUNDARY

As early as 2000 B.C., God asked Job: "Who shut up the sea with doors . . . and marked out for it my bound, And set bars and doors, And said, Hitherto shalt thou come, but no further; And here shall thy proud waves be stayed?" (Job 38:8-11). Scripture places great emphasis upon God's *covenant of the rainbow* with the human race: "the waters shall no more become a flood to destroy all flesh" (Gen. 9:15), thereby emphasizing also the uniqueness of the Deluge as a *global catastrophe.* If the Flood was limited in extent, the rainbow covenant has failed, for there have been hundreds of devastating local floods since then!

About 1000 B.C., the promise was confirmed: "Thou hast set a bound that they may not pass over; that they turn not again to cover the earth" (Ps. 104:9). About 700 B.C., the promise was confirmed again: "For this is as the waters of Noah unto me; for as I have sworn that the waters of Noah shall no more go over the earth, so have I sworn that I will not be wroth with thee, nor rebuke thee" (Isa. 54:9). Finally, about 600 B.C., the promise was confirmed yet again: "Fear ye not me? saith Jehovah: will ye not tremble at my presence, who have placed the sand for the bound of the sea, by a perpetual decree, that it cannot pass it? and though the waves thereof toss themselves, yet can they not prevail; though they roar, yet can they not pass over it" (Jer. 5:22).

One such flood was sufficient to demonstrate forever the sovereignty and holiness and power of God as the Judge of all mankind (Gen. 8:21, Ps. 29:10), and therefore the world will never see another like it.

Genesis 9, in which God assured mankind that there would *never again* be a universal Flood (cf. Isa. 54:9).

Now the key statement in this passage (Ps. 104:8) for our purposes is in the beginning of verse 8: "The mountains rose, the valleys sank down" (ASV; cf. RSV, Berkeley, Amplified, NASB). We have already seen in Genesis 8:2 that the ocean basins were lowered at the termination of the Flood, and with this concept the phrase *"the valleys sank down"* is in agreement. God supernaturally depressed various parts of the earth's crust, and into those places which God "founded for them" the waters "fled" and "hasted away," there to abide while this earth exists (cf. Rev. 21:1), never again to cover the continents.

Some Bible students have denied that Psalm 104:6-9 can refer to the Flood and to the Rainbow Covenant because of its similarity to such passages as Job 38:8-11, Psalm 33:7, Proverbs 8:22-31, and Jeremiah 5:22, which seem to speak of the original lifting up of continents from the oceans during the Creation Week (Gen. 1:9). Of course, if continents have arisen from the sea on two separate occasions, we could expect to find similar expressions to describe these geologic crises. But there are at least two important distinctions made in Scripture between these events. First, the original oceans *did not cover previously existing mountains* (contrast Psalm 104:6—"the waters stood above the mountains"). Secondly, the original oceans *were not bound by a perpetual decree* (contrast Psalm 104:9—"that they turn not again to cover the earth").[31]

The Formation of Our Present Mountain Ranges

It is important to observe that Psalm 104:6-9 adds one idea that is only implied in the Genesis account. Not only were new and deeper ocean basins formed, but also *"the mountains rose."* This cannot refer simply to mountain peaks appearing to rise as the waters subsided, as if the passage were given from Noah's personal viewpoint as he peered from the window of the Ark. Otherwise, the parallel phrase "the

---

31. In the light of these distinctions, we may say that Job 38:8-11 could refer to the original oceans because no perpetual decree is mentioned (on the other hand, the mention of "the cloud" in vs. 9 suggests a post-Flood phenomenon, and vs. 12 could be speaking of the decree of Gen. 8:22). Psalm 33:7 and Proverbs 8:22-31 do seem to refer to a Creation Week event, but no mention is made of a perpetual decree (cf. Prov. 8:29). For this reason, and because of its similarity to Isaiah 54:9, Jeremiah 5:22 must refer to the great Flood of Noah's day.

valleys sank down" would have no meaning, and the obvious connection with Genesis 8:3 would be broken.

Psalm 104:8 is actually saying that God supernaturally pushed up great mountain ranges in the continental areas to balance the new depths in the ocean basins. Thus, global topography, as we see it today, was not shaped by an accumulation of infinitesimal changes through vast periods of time, as the uniformitarian, Lyellian[32] approach to mountain-building would insist, but rather by a sudden and stupendous work of God, whereby new continents emerged from the universal waters and sedimentary strata (formed by the vast complex of currents during the Flood year) were lifted thousands of feet above sea level in the mountainous regions of the earth.[33]

Such an interpretation of Psalm 104:8 incidentally solves one of the great problems connected with a universal Flood concept. It is frequently maintained, and rightfully so, that there simply is not enough water in our present oceans to cover all the mountains of the earth, even if ocean basins could somehow be pushed up to present sea levels, for there are many mountains more than 20,000 feet high, with an average of only 12,000 feet of water to cover them. But if these mountains (with their marine fossils) rose to their present heights *since* the Flood, we may assume that none of the "high mountains" that existed before the Flood (Gen. 7:19) were more than 6,000 to 7,000 feet high.

Conclusion

If the basic supernaturalism of the Flood, as set forth in these various passages of Scripture, is to be taken seriously by the evangelical Christian, *he must to that extent part company with the standard approach of historical geologists to the past history of our planet.* Such an approach com-

---

32. In the early nineteenth century Charles Lyell popularized the "uniformitarian" approach to earth history—that geomorphic processes which can be observed in action at present, such as erosion, sedimentation, glaciation, volcanism, diastrophism, etc. (all operating in *essentially* the same fashion as at present) can be invoked to explain the origin and formation of *all* the earth's geologic features. Compare definitions of uniformitarianism and catastrophism in Whitcomb and Morris, *The Genesis Flood,* pp. xx, xxi, 131, 137; and R. Hooykaas, *The Principle of Uniformity in Geology, Biology and Theology* (Leiden: E. J. Brill, 1963), pp. 30-31. Also, see below, pp. 99-106 ff.

33. Uniformitarianism simply cannot explain mountain-building. See *The Genesis Flood,* pp. 140-42; and Immanuel Velikovsky, *Earth in Upheaval* (New York: Dell Pub. Co., reprinted 1965), pp. 70-92.

HIGH MOUNTAINS SINCE THE FLOOD

Enormously high, snow-capped mountain peaks could not have existed before the Flood. "The world that perished" had low-lying mountains which were probably less than six or seven thousand feet high, because they were completely covered by the waters of the Flood ("all the high mountains that were under the whole heaven were covered . . . the mountains were covered"—Gen. 7:19-20). If the earth's surface had no irregularities at all, the oceans would cover it to a depth of about two miles. Therefore, if Mount Ararat, which is more than three miles high (or Mount Everest, which is more than five miles high), existed *before* the Flood at such altitudes, it could not have been covered by the Flood.

Scripture tells us that it was not until *after* the Flood that "the mountains rose" (Ps. 104:8). Their rise to great heights was both sudden and supernatural, for the immediate effect of God's intervention was that the waters "fled . . . they hasted away . . . Unto the place which thou hadst founded for them" (Ps. 104:7-8). Uniformitarian geologists have searched in vain for the forces necessary to raise up the great mountain ranges of the world (cf. Whitcomb and Morris, *The Genesis Flood,* pp. 140-42). Geologic evidence for the sudden and recent rise of Mount Ararat is presented by Clifford L. Burdick, "Ararat—The Mother of Mountains," *Creation Research Society Quarterly,* June, 1967, pp. 5-12.

pletely ignores the Genesis account of this world-wide catastrophe, and seeks to explain the earth's geologic and paleontologic features in terms of the uniformist principle.

The Flood constitutes a sharp line of demarcation between our present world, with its basically uniform cycle of seedtime and harvest, cold and heat, summer and winter, and day and night (Gen. 8:22), and "the world that then was," with its low-lying, fossil-free and ice-free mountains, its rainless sky and universally warm and humid climate, and its shallow seas. The transformation that ended that world and started this world was as sudden and supernaturally cataclysmic as the change that shall end this present world and inaugurate the "new heaven" and "new earth" of Revelation 21:1. Our present world of natural processes, therefore, so far from being the proper scientific standard for judging and measuring the eternal past and future, is a unique cosmic interlude hemmed in by universal waters on the one side and universal fires on the other. As Christians who desire to honor God and His Word, let us not be found guilty of making void this infallible written Word through the traditions of men (cf. Mark 7:7-8) as we seek to interpret the Biblical account of the Flood.

2
the flood destroyed the entire world

I F IT BE granted that Scripture gives clear indication of the supernatural origin and termination of the Flood, a major objection to its geographical universality is thereby removed. For apart from such stupendous miracles, it is certainly true that there could have been no such catastrophe. However, there are a number of evangelical interpreters who are willing to grant that such miracles occurred, and yet they hesitate to affirm that the Bible definitely teaches that the Deluge covered the entire globe. There are various reasons for this hesitation, most of them based upon supposed geological objections; but before we consider the geological aspects of the Flood, we must review the Biblical evidences for its universality.

The Depth of the Flood

Perhaps the most important evidence for the universality of the Flood is the statement of Genesis 7:19-20 ("and the waters prevailed exceedingly upon the earth; and all the high mountains that were under the whole heaven were covered"). Obviously, if only *one* high mountain were covered with water for only *a week,* the Flood waters, in order to maintain such a depth, would have had to reach a similar depth everywhere else on the planet because of the force of gravity. But that *not even one mountain peak* remained above the surface is indicated in Genesis 7:20 ("Fifteen cubits upward did the waters prevail; and the mountains were covered"). Most commentators agree that the fifteen cubits (about 22 feet) must have reference to Noah's Ark, which had a draught of about fifteen cubits, or half its height. Thus, the highest mountains were covered by at least this depth during the 110 days in which the waters "prevailed" upon the earth, or else the Ark would have been destroyed upon one of the mountains.

Arthur Custance has objected to such an interpretation, for if the Flood covered the mountains, the "rarified atmosphere" at elevations above that of Mount Everest would "render all but a few creatures insensible in a very few moments for lack of oxygen."[1] He particularly expresses concern about Noah and his sons having to climb between the Ark's three decks at such high elevations. But all such concerns are misplaced, for it is an elementary fact that atmospheric pressure depends on elevation *relative to sea level*. The air column above the raised sea level during the

---

1. Custance, *The Extent of the Flood,* p. 9.

Flood was just as high, and the resulting sea level atmospheric pressure just as great, as the present sea level pressure.

The Duration of the Flood

While there may be some difference of opinion as to the exact depth of the Flood (depending upon the altitude of antediluvian mountains), there can be *no* question as to its duration. Scripture informs us that the Flood attained its maximum, mountain-covering depth in *six weeks,* and continued to cover "all the high mountains that were under the whole heaven" for *an additional sixteen weeks.*

One hundred and fifty days after the Flood began, the waters started to subside and the Ark grounded on one of the highest mountain peaks (for the Ark grounded on the very same day the waters began to assuage—Gen. 7:11; 8:3-4). However, *ten weeks* later, nothing could be seen above the water level except other mountain peaks (8:4-5)! And still another *twenty-one weeks* were required for the waters to subside sufficiently for Noah to disembark safely *in the mountains of Ararat!* How a flood of such depth and duration could have covered only a limited portion of the earth's surface has never been satisfactorily explained.

Arthur Kuschke, Jr., who holds to the local Flood view, simply dismisses all of these arguments as having no validity. "A physical event," he informs us, "caused waters to flood the land. But we simply cannot describe the character or degree or extent of this physical event; the Bible does not tell us. The Bible says the waters rose, and the waters later receded; but it is silent respecting immense tidal waves. Except for Noah and his family, the flood destroyed the human race; but we do not know whether it covered the entire globe."[2] The burden of proof, of course, rests upon those who maintain that a year-long, mountain-covering flood could have remained local in extent! It is difficult to imagine what more the Bible could have said to emphasize the universality of the Deluge.

The Need for an Ark

In discussing the dimensions of the Ark, we have already demonstrated how appropriate these were for the purpose that this structure was to serve.[3] But to look at the matter

---

2. Arthur W. Kuschke, Jr., review of *The Genesis Flood,* in *Westminster Theological Journal,* May, 1962, p. 220. Reprinted in *JASA,* June, 1964, p. 62.
3. See above, pp. 22 ff.

from a different standpoint, wholly apart from the question of the exact size of the Ark, *there would have been no need for an Ark at all if the flood was local in extent!* The whole procedure of constructing such a vessel, involving over 100 years of planning and toiling, simply to escape a local flood can hardly be described as anything but utterly foolish and unnecessary! How much more sensible it would have been for God simply to have warned Noah of the coming destruction in plenty of time for him to move to an area that would not have been affected by the Flood, even as Lot was taken out of Sodom before the fire fell from heaven. Not only so, but also the great numbers of animals of all kinds, and certainly the birds, could easily have moved out of the danger zone also, without having to be stored in a barge for an entire year! The Biblical record simply cannot be harmonized with the concept of a Flood that was confined to the Near East.

And yet, in spite of the apparently irresistible force of this argument for a global Flood, we find evangelical scholars who promote the local Flood view discussing the design and dimensions and capacity and purpose of the Ark with little apparent appreciation of the basic inconsistency of such a study! One would think that the Biblical description of the Ark would be by-passed in embarrassed silence by men whose view of the Flood would bring into serious question *the need for an Ark at all,* to say nothing of an Ark of such enormous dimensions.

R. Laird Harris, for example, begins his discussion of the Ark by pointing out that "the building of the ark and the building of the tower of Babel are the two first major enterprises of man according to the Bible."[4] He then discusses its possible diamond-shaped cross section,[5] the tools that were probably available for the task, the 100,000 square feet of deck space, and the number of animals that could be accommodated. *But what about the Flood that this Ark was designed to survive?* Dr. Harris writes:

> Bible students may have been viewing the flood too simply. The Bible gives few details, but speaks of movements in the ocean bottom raising the water levels of the world along with torrential rains. Actually the Hebrew word *flood* (used

4. R. Laird Harris, *Man—God's Eternal Creation* (Chicago: Moody Press, 1971), p. 87.
5. Based on Meir Ben Uri's speculative model. Cf. *Time,* Feb. 23, 1968, pp. 76, 79; and *Christianity Today,* March 29, 1968, pp. 666-67.

only in Genesis and Psalm 29:10) is the word meaning "storm." Is it not possible that the storm was a rainstorm in the Mesopotamian locality and other lower latitudes and a snowstorm on the mountains and in Siberia and northern regions? The tops of the mountains on this view were hidden by the storm and covered with snow. Of course in such a deep snow lasting for most of a year, "all flesh, wherein is the breath of life" (Gen. 6:17) would die either from the cold or by starvation. However, such a combination of flood, rain, and snowstorm would not upset the balance of nature nor kill fish or plant life. Such a flood would explain the Siberian mammoths and the death of all living men outside the ark and yet it would allow for the preservation of the bones and artifacts of the antediluvian men.[6]

In analyzing this statement, we would ask just two questions. First, how could "a rainstorm in the Mesopotamian locality and other lower latitudes and a snowstorm on the mountains and in Siberia and northern regions" explain "the death of all living men outside the ark"? And secondly, if pre-Flood geography was basically the same as today (an assumption shared by all local Flood advocates), could not Noah and his family have been warned by God to move to Africa or India to escape this "rainstorm" and "snowstorm" and thus avoid the necessity of spending a hundred years constructing an Ark with 100,000 square feet of deck space?

In his various writings, Dr. Harris has made some outstanding contributions to Christian apologetics. But when he states that "the tops of the mountains on this view were hidden by the storm and covered with snow," he approaches the dangerous view that Noah erroneously *thought* that the highest mountains were covered by the Flood! But Genesis 7:19-20 is the inspired record of *God's explanations, not Noah's opinions.*[7] This passage clearly indicates that the

6. Harris, *Man—God's Eternal Creation,* p. 85. Three years earlier, however, Dr. Harris was able to state: "The writer, for one, does believe in a flood of universal extent" ("The Mist, the Canopy, and the Rivers of Eden," p. 179).

7. See below, pp. 59-63. T. C. Mitchell (art. "Flood," in *The New Bible Dictionary;* London: The Inter-Varsity Fellowship, 1962, p. 427) limits all the universal terms in the Flood narrative by assuming that the narrator was so confused by "the cloud and mist that must have accompanied the cataclysm" that the *thought* all the high mountains under the whole heaven were covered. For a more Biblical perspective on the Flood, see Francis A. Schaeffer, *Genesis in Space and Time* (Downers Grove, Ill.: Inter-Varsity Press, 1972), pp. 129-40.

same waters which lifted up the Ark also covered the mountains and that the Ark was carried by the waters until it was left on "the mountains of Ararat" (8:4). A snowstorm in the mountains would not have done this! Furthermore, it is clear from Genesis 7:22-23 that the purpose of the Ark was to save eight human beings and the animals from death by *drowning,* not from starvation and freezing.

Dr. Filby devotes fourteen pages of his book to a study of Noah's Ark, and includes much worthwhile material as well as some mere speculations.[8] But he falls far short of demonstrating why such a structure was really *needed* on the basis of a limited Flood. For a moment, Filby actually toys with the possibility of a *global* catastrophe: "Perhaps there is the faintest suggestion that the upheaval which caused the Flood was so vast that for a short time it altered or threatened the stability of the very seasons."[9] Furthermore, "while all agree that the poles have in the past slowly wandered *no geologist is prepared to admit a wholesale sudden shift in the polar axis in the Pleistocene period.* Yet the strange stories of the mammoths and the bone caves, and the curious characters of lakes and seas like the Caspian and Aral and Van, the peculiarities of lakes high up in the Andes, the vast smashed forests and buried animal remains of the Arctic Islands *and numerous other phenomena of like kind scattered across the world make one pause.*"[10] But—unswerving loyalty to the currently popular concepts of uniformitarian geology[11] leaves Dr. Filby at the "almost persuaded" level

---

8. Filby, *The Flood Reconsidered,* pp. 86-101. While admitting that the Ark could have carried as much as *15,000 tons of cargo,* Filby speculates that only *100 tons of animals* needed to be on board, with the rest of the tonnage reserved for food and water (pp. 88, 96)! But even if we accept this fantastically low figure, would it really have been "perfectly reasonable for Noah to collect and eight people to care for" (p. 86) even 100 tons (200,000 pounds) of animals in the Ark for a year without God's *direct* intervention? We think not.
9. Filby, pp. 120-21.
10. Filby, p. 121. Italics added. Whatever may be said for a shift of the polar axis, there are many events *clearly taught in Scripture,* both supernatural and catastrophic, which few geologists are "prepared to admit" because of very deep-seated uniformitarian presuppositions. See below, pp. 99 ff.
11. Filby, pp. 2-3. A fellow-Britisher, David C. C. Watson keenly observes: "Filby appears to accept the standard geological column as sacrosanct because it is drawn up by professional geologists, but when he comes to archaeology and Near East geology, he is prepared to back his own (amateur) opinion against a host of professionals. . . . He seems not to realize that *all* modern science and

and with the disappointing confession: "At present it is better to take *the only reasonable course* and confess that *we just do not know*. We leave the question open."[12] Retreating back to the local Flood view, Dr. Filby thereby leaves unanswered that vital and persistent question that will not be silenced—*Why build an Ark at all?*

Surely one of the most astonishing examples of logical and theological inconsistency in our day is the rejection of "Morris and Whitcomb's universal Flood theory" by an evangelical theologian who nevertheless defends the inerrancy of Scripture in public debates and carries on explorations above the 12,000 foot level of Mt. Ararat to discover the remains of Noah's Ark![13] Dr. John Warwick Montgomery is convinced that world evangelism would be greatly simplified if we could just discover the Ark. "The missionary value of the find would be staggering, if only on the level of providing a common ground for the general presentation of the biblical message. Beginning with Turkey itself . . . opportunities for active discussion of the scriptural message would certainly accompany the news of the find in all parts of the world. Moreover . . . those who are touched by [the story of the Ark] can experience genuine pre-evangelism."[14]

One cannot help but wonder, however, at the type of "pre-evangelism" that points to remains of Noah's Ark high on Mount Ararat *and then denies the Biblical testimony to the global Flood that put it there!* Dr. Montgomery cries out: "We couldn't stand the strain of Ararat if the winds of unbelief in the authority of God's Holy Word didn't impel us to do all that is possible to confirm its entire trustworthi-

---

scholarship is bedeviled by blindness at the fact of the Flood, so that they misinterpret *all* the phenomena—whether in geology, archaeology, or anthropology. . . . Taken as a whole, Dr. Filby's book shows how untenable is a middle position on the Flood: we must *either* accept Genesis 7-9 at its face value *or* agree with the critics that it is pure legend." (*Creation Research Society Quarterly,* June, 1971, pp. 54, 80).

12. Filby, p. 121. Italics added. To leave questions open and unanswered when Scripture speaks clearly is far from being "the only reasonable course." Agnosticism is no virtue in the presence of a "thus saith the Lord." See Matthew 21:27.

13. John Warwick Montgomery, *The Quest For Noah's Ark* (Minneapolis: Bethany Fellowship, Inc., 1972), pp. 41, 263. See also his articles in *Christianity Today:* "Ark Fever," July 2, 1971, pp. 946-47; "A Question of Credentials," August 27, 1971, p. 1043; "Arkeology 1971," January 7, 1972, pp. 342-43; and "How Not to Find the Ark," December 22, 1972, p. 326.

14. Montgomery, *The Quest for Noah's Ark,* p. 274.

ness."[15] But is not the Bible *entirely trustworthy as it now stands,* in its clear witness to Noah's Ark *and* a universal Flood? Did not our Lord explain that "if they hear not Moses and the prophets, neither will they be persuaded, if one rise from the dead" (Luke 16:31)? Would people who now reject the authority of God's Word truly acknowledge it, even if remains of the Ark were discovered?

Dr. Montgomery's zeal in searching for archaeological evidences that agree with Biblical facts is indeed commendable. But it is highly inconsistent for a Christian archaeologist to seek the "confirmation" of some Biblical facts (e.g., the Ark) while rejecting other Biblical facts (e.g., the global Flood)! Dr. Montgomery's problem (which he shares with many Christian theologians and scientists today) traces back to his early indoctrination in a uniformitarian approach to earth history. He writes of a certain teacher at the Cornell University Space Center "toward whom I admit an especially powerful bias, since he was instrumental in my conversion to Christianity while an obstreperous philosophy major at Cornell."[16] It is perfectly understandable that one would experience a powerful bias toward the viewpoints of a skillful teacher. But the vital question is this: Ought not a Christian subject all human opinions to the absolute standards of God's Word? Ought not a Christian rather admit to "an especially powerful bias" toward the clear statements of Moses, Peter, and the Lord Jesus Christ Himself concerning the magnitude of the Flood?

It may have been this powerful bias that led Dr. Montgomery to make a caricature of *The Genesis Flood* rather than to read the arguments of the book carefully:

> "The world was created in 4004 B.C., but with built-in evidence of radiocarbon dating, fossil evidence, etc., indicating millions of years of prior developmental growth." This assertion, given current popularity by Whitcomb and Morris in their controversial, anti-evolutionary book, *The Genesis Flood,* is a nonsensical proposition. Why? Because it excludes all possible testability.... Moreover, the statement is reconcilable with an infinite number of parallel assertions, such as "The world was created ten years ago (or ten minutes ago) with built-in history."[17]

---

15. Montgomery, "Arkeology 1971," p. 343.
16. John W. Montgomery, "How Scientific Is Science?" *Christianity Today,* September 29, 1972, p. 52. Note Roger Schmurr's comment in a Letter to the Editor, November 10, 1972, p. 48.
17. John W. Montgomery, "Inspiration and Inerrancy: A New Depart-

This statement constitutes a serious blunder in evangelical scholarship. Even a cursory reading of *The Genesis Flood* reveals none of these positions. The authors would agree wholeheartedly with Dr. Montgomery that any view of creation which assumes that the earth could have been created ten years ago would indeed be meaningless, because such a proposition is *clearly denied by Scripture* (which can and has stood the acid test of objective verifiability), which calls for an earth created *at least* six thousand years ago.[18] Furthermore, on the basis of Scriptural indications of gaps in the genealogies of Genesis 5 and 11 (as carefully explained in the final chapter of *The Genesis Flood*), the authors believe that Creation occurred thousands (but not tens of thousands) of years *before* 4004 B.C. Even more important, the book constantly asserts that fossils in the crust of the earth, so far from having been created *in situ,* are the effects of catastrophes, especially the millions of complex currents that swirled over the earth during the year-long Deluge described in Genesis 6-9.

The reason why the position set forth in *The Genesis Flood* is not "analytically meaningless" (to use Dr. Montgomery's expression)[19] is that it can be verified in the inerrant Scriptures which teach that the Flood was geographically universal. This view can also be verified hydrodynamically and paleontologically in the unbelievably vast fossiliferous strata in every continent, which demand a catastrophic rather than a uniformitarian interpretation.[20] There is also a wide variety of power scientific evidences for a comparatively recent creation of the earth.[21] The authors do *not* appeal to the idea of "built-in evidence of radiocarbon dating" to harmonize Scripture with science, as may be seen from a check on the index references to radiocarbon dating.

To summarize our discussion, the necessity of an Ark to save air-breathing creatures through the Flood is absolutely

ture," *Bulletin of the Evangelical Theological Society,* Vol. 8, No. 2 (Spring, 1965), p. 59.
18. For a discussion of the Biblical doctrine of creation with a superficial appearance of history, see J. C. Whitcomb, *The Early Earth* (Grand Rapids: Baker Book House, 1972), pp. 29-38.
19. Montgomery, "Inspiration," p. 63.
20. See below, pp. 71-92.
21. For an impressive collection of such evidences, the reader is referred to two volumes edited by Dr. Walter E. Lammerts: *Why Not Creation?* and *Scientific Studies in Special Creation* (Nutley, N.J.: Presbyterian and Reformed Pub. Co., 1970 and 1971). See also Melvin A. Cook, *Prehistory and Earth Models* (London: Max Parrish and Co., Ltd., 1966), pp. 340-41.

devastating to any compromising position with regard to the extent of the Flood. Even if only a small portion of the earth escaped the Deluge, there would have been no need for an Ark at all. And to claim that the remains of the Ark probably exist above the 12,000 foot level of Mt. Ararat, while at the same time insisting that it was placed there by a local flood, is to claim the impossible. The only acceptable solution is to take the Scriptures for what they say—the Flood covered the entire earth.

The Total Destruction of a Widely Distributed Human Race

From the very beginning of the modern Flood controversy over 140 years ago, there has been little question among conservative Christian scholars as to the total destruction of the human race by the Flood.[22] There are four basic reasons for this general consensus.

First, the Flood must have destroyed the entire human race outside the Ark because the Scriptures state that the purpose of the Flood was to wipe out a sinful and degenerate humanity, and this purpose could not have been accomplished by destroying only a portion of mankind (Gen. 6:5-7, 11-13).

Second, there are repeated statements to the effect that Noah and his family were the *only* ones who escaped the judgment waters (Gen. 6:8-9, 17-18; 7:1; I Peter 3:20; II Peter 2:5).

Third, the Lord Jesus Christ stated that the Flood destroyed *all* men except Noah's family, just as the fire destroyed *all* Sodomites except Lot's family (Luke 17:26-30; cf. Matt. 24:39).

Fourth, the covenant of the rainbow in Genesis 9 obviously applies to the entire human race; but the Scriptures repeatedly state that God made this covenant with Noah and his sons. Therefore, the whole of humanity has descended from Noah's family, and the Flood destroyed the entire antediluvian world of men.

Those who acknowledge the tremendous weight of Biblical testimony concerning the total destruction of mankind outside of the Ark, and yet remain unwilling to admit that the Flood was geographically universal, usually maintain that mankind had not spread beyond the limits of Mesopotamia during the period from Adam to Noah. But it is our con-

---

22. Cf. Whitcomb and Morris, *The Genesis Flood,* pp. 36-54, for an extensive analysis of Bernard Ramm's concept of an anthropologically local flood.

THE OCEAN — GOD'S INSTRUMENT OF GLOBAL JUDGMENT

More than 70 percent of the earth's surface is covered with water, making planet Earth unique in the entire known universe, where nearly all of the matter consists of either flaming gasses or frozen solids. In places the ocean is far deeper (more than 35,000 feet in one part of the western Pacific) than the highest mountain. The sea contains 330 million cubic miles of water. This is enough "to fill a standpipe 75 miles in diameter and 70,000 miles high — which is approximately one third the distance from the earth to the moon" (Leonard Engel, *The Sea;* New York: Time Incorporated, 1961, p. 11).

If the earth's surface were made completely even, it would everywhere be covered by approximately 12,000 feet of water. Thus, when we read that "the fountains of the great deep" were broken up in the early phase of the Flood year (Gen. 7:11) in such a way that ocean basins pushed their waters over the highest mountains of the continents within six weeks, we have a clear indication that mountains before the Flood were much lower than those of our present world. We have no way of knowing how high "the waters stood above the mountains" (Ps. 104:6), but it was by a depth of *at least* 15 cubits (22 feet) in order that Noah's Ark, settling about half its 30-cubit height into the water, might be protected from destruction during the months that it floated upon the shoreless ocean (Gen. 7:20).

Never again will the ocean serve as God's instrument of global judgment. The rainbow covenant of Genesis 9 is His guarantee to the human race of this fact. But it does serve as a wholesome reminder to proud and careless men that God — not man — is sovereign in all the world. The fact that God's voice once thundered "upon many waters" while He "sat as King at the Flood" is sufficient warning to the human race to "ascribe unto Jehovah glory and strength . . . the glory due unto his name," for He "sitteth as King for ever" (Ps. 29:1-3, 10).

viction that such a position cannot be successfully defended for at least four reasons.

In the first place, the remarkable longevity and fecundity of the antediluvians strongly imply a rapid increase of population during the *minimum* of 1,656 years that elapsed between Adam and the Flood.[23] Secondly, the prevalence of strife and violence among men before the Flood suggests a wide distribution of peoples, rather than a confinement to a single locality. The history of Indian tribes on our own continent is an obvious illustration of this point. Twice in one chapter the Bible emphasizes this idea: "the earth was filled with violence" (Gen. 6:11, 13). Note that these verses do not simply report that there was violence in the earth, but that *the earth was filled with it!* Thirdly, the evidence of human fossil remains in widely scattered areas of the earth, some of which may well be antediluvian, makes it even more difficult to maintain that men did not migrate beyond the Mesopotamian Valley before the time of the Flood.[24] And finally, "man would not have needed to spread very far before *some* would have occupied high ground and thus requiring a Flood of considerable depth and, logically, global extent."[25]

The Testimony of the Apostle Peter

One of the most important Biblical passages relating to the magnitude of the Deluge is found in II Peter 3:3-7.

> ...knowing this first, that in the last days mockers shall come with mockery, walking after their own lusts, and saying, Where is the promise of his coming? for, from the day that the fathers fell asleep, all things continue as they were from the beginning of the creation. For this they wilfully forget, that there were heavens from of old, and an earth compacted out of the water and amidst water, by the word of God; by which means the world that then was, being overflowed with water, perished: but the heavens that now

23. Cf. Henry M. Morris, *Biblical Cosmology and Modern Science* (Grand Rapids: Baker Book House, 1970), pp. 77-79.
24. For a helpful discussion of human fossil remains, see Arthur C. Custance, "Fossil Man in the Light of the Record in Genesis," in *Why Not Creation?* ed. by Walter Lammerts (Nutley, N.J.: Presbyterian and Reformed Pub. Co., 1970), pp. 194-229. Also, "The Origin of Man," Chapter 5 in *Evolution: The Fossils Say No!* by Duane T. Gish (San Diego: Institute for Creation Research, 1972).
25. Charles A. Clough, "A Calm Appraisal of *The Genesis Flood*," (Unpublished Th.M. thesis, Dallas Theological Seminary, 1968), p. 53.

of the apostle Peter. It was the Flood that utilized the vast oceans of water out of which and amidst which the ancient earth was "compacted," unto the utter destruction of the *kosmos* "that then was." It was the Flood to which Peter appealed as his final and incontrovertible answer to those who chose to remain in willful ignorance of the fact that God had *at one time* in the past demonstrated His holy wrath and omnipotence by subjecting "all things" to an overwhelming, cosmic catastrophe that was on an absolute par with the final day of judgment, in which God will yet consume the earth with fire and cause the very elements to dissolve with fervent heat (II Peter 3:10).

If the Flood was limited to the region of Mesopotamia (or even beyond),[26] it is difficult to see how Peter's appeal to the Flood would have any value as a contradiction to the doctrine of total uniformitarianism, which assumes that "all things" have *never yet* been upset by a supernatural and universal cataclysm. Nor is it easy to excuse Peter of gross exaggeration and inaccuracy when he depicted the Flood in such cosmic terms and in such an absolutely universal context, if it was only a local inundation after all.

Strange indeed, in the light of this, are the words of Derek Kidner, a prominent British advocate of the local Flood theory:

> ... we should be careful to read the (Flood) account wholeheartedly in its own terms, which depict a *total* judgment on the ungodly world already set before us in Genesis—not an event of debatable dimensions in a world we may try to reconstruct. The whole living scene is blotted out, and the New Testament makes us learn from it the greater judgment that awaits not only our entire globe but the universe itself (II Peter 3:5-7).[27]

If "the New Testament makes us learn" from the Genesis

---

26. Dr. Filby concedes that the Flood must have "swept from the Atlantic, the Mediterranean, and the Indian Oceans over much of Europe and Asia to Alaska and even beyond"! (*The Flood Reconsidered*, pp. 31-32). He even quotes with apparent approval (p. 35, note No. 36) a statement by Patrick O'Connell in *Science of Today and the Problems of Genesis* (St. Paul, Minn.: Radio Replies Press Society, 1959) that the Flood must also have covered India, China, and North America east of the Rocky Mountains. But if one comes this close to accepting the Biblical testimony to a universal Flood, why not come all the way?

27. Derek Kidner, *Genesis: An Introduction and Commentary* (Chicago: Inter-Varsity Press, 1967), p. 95.

are, and the earth, by the same word have been stored up for fire, being reserved against the day of judgment and destruction of ungodly men.

In this passage of Scripture, the apostle Peter spoke of a day, yet future from his standpoint, when men would no longer think seriously of Christ's Second Coming as a cataclysmic, universal intervention by God into the course of world affairs. And the reason for this skeptical attitude would be none other than a blind adherence to *the doctrine of total uniformitarianism*—a doctrine which maintains that *natural laws and processes have never yet been interrupted so as to bring about a total destruction of human civilization through the direct intervention of God.* And since (we are told) this has never been the case in past history, there should be no cause to fear that it will ever occur in the future!

In answering these skeptics of the end-time, Peter pointed to two events in the past which cannot be explained on the basis of uniformitarianism. The first of these events was the creation of the world: "there were heavens from of old, and an earth . . . *by the word of God*"; and the second event was the Flood: "the world *(kosmos)* that then was, being overflowed with water, perished *(apōleto)*."

But it was the second of these two events, the Flood, which served as the basis for Peter's comparison with the Second Coming and the final destruction of the world. For even as "the world that then was" perished by *water,* so "the heavens that now are, and the earth," have been "stored up for *fire,* being reserved against the day of judgment and destruction of ungodly men."

Let us now consider the implication of this passage with respect to the geographical extent of the Flood. In speaking of the events of the second and third days of creation, Peter used the terms "heavens *from of old,* and an earth" in a sense that is obviously universal. By the same token, no one can deny that Peter also used the terms "heavens *that now are,* and the earth" in the strictly universal sense. Otherwise, Peter would have been speaking of the creation and final destruction of only a part of the earth!

The one event which Peter set forth as having brought about a transformation, not of the earth only but also of the very *heavens,* was the Flood! It was the Flood that constituted the line of demarcation between "the heavens from of old" and "the heavens that now are" in the thinkin

Flood account that the coming judgment will involve "not only our entire globe but the universe itself," one must ask how this lesson can be learned from a Flood that was only local in extent.

Thus, the third chapter of II Peter provides powerful New Testament support for the geographical universality of the Deluge. Anything less than a catastrophe of such proportions would upset the entire force of the apostle's argument and would give much encouragement to those who would teach what he so solemnly condemned.

The Problem of Universal Terms

It has frequently been argued by advocates of a limited Flood that such terms as "all" and "every" need not be understood in the strictly universal sense. For example, when we read in Genesis 41:57 that *"all* countries came into Egypt to buy grain," we need not interpret this as meaning that representatives from South America and Australia were among those who came to Egypt. Therefore, when Genesis 7:19 tells us that *"all* the high mountains that were under the *whole* heaven were covered," and that *"all* in whose nostrils was the breath of the spirit of life, of *all* that was on dry land, died" (v. 22), we are at liberty to understand these universal terms in a limited sense, and thus are justified from a Biblical standpoint in advocating a geographically local Flood.

In spite of the seeming logic of this argument, there are several considerations that render it untenable. In the first place, the great majority of passages in the Bible where these terms are employed demand the universal usage. For example, Jesus said to his disciples: *"All* authority hath been given unto me in heaven and on earth. Go ye therefore, and make disciples of *all* the nations . . . teaching them to observe *all* things whatsoever I commanded you" (Matt. 28:18-20). The Bible is filled with statements that lose their meaning on the limited usage interpretation.

This leads to our second observation. The only possible way to determine the sense in which universal terms are to be understood is to examine the immediate and general *context* in which they are used. Let us therefore examine the Biblical context for the Flood account of Genesis 6-9. The Book of Genesis is clearly divided into two main sections: (1) chapters 1-11 deal with *universal* origins (the material universe, plants, animals, human beings, sin, redemption, and the nations of the earth); (2) chapters 12-50, on the other hand, concentrate upon the *particular* origin of the Hebrew nation and its tribes, mentioning other nations only insofar as they came into contact with Israel. A realization of this fact sheds important light on the question of the magnitude of the Flood, for the Biblical account of this catastrophe occupies *three and a half chapters* in the midst of these eleven chapters which deal with universal origins, while only *two* chapters are devoted to the creation of all things!

From a purely literary and historical perspective, therefore, we are perfectly justified in coming to the account of the Flood in Genesis 6-9 with the expectation of reading about *a catastrophe of world-wide proportions.* And if we are willing to come to Scripture with a mind conditioned by perspectives that the Word of God itself supplies for us, unencumbered with uniformitarian presuppositions, we will not be surprised to discover that the number of Hebrew superlatives used to describe the magnitude of the Deluge is entirely proportional to the amount of space allotted to it in the first eleven chapters of Genesis.

Our third observation is that the universal terms of Genesis 6-9 cannot be understood in a limited sense, because *the physical phenomena* described in these chapters would be utterly inconceivable if the Flood had been confined to the Mesopotamian Valley or even to the Near East. While it would be entirely possible for a seven-year famine to grip the entire Near East without affecting South America (cf. Gen. 41:57), it would *not* be possible for water to cover the high mountains of the Near East for even a *week* without disastrously affecting South America as well!

So we will agree that the words "all" and "every" must be understood in the light of their *context;* but so far from disproving the geographical universality of the Flood, *this hermeneutical principle actually establishes it.* It is really quite futile to speak of the Flood as being "universal in so far as the area and observation and information of the narrator extended."[28] There is nothing in the entire passage of Genesis 6-9 to indicate that Noah is giving his personal impressions of the Flood. Instead, it is all seen from God's viewpoint. Noah does not speak a single word in the entire account until the very end of the ninth chapter when *God* put into his mouth the remarkable prophecy concerning his three sons. One might just as reasonably argue that the

---

28. Ramm, *The Christian View,* p. 240.

creation narrative of Genesis 1 only applies to part of the earth because of Adam's limited experience. Thus, when Dr. Filby asks, "What, in fact, was the 'earth' which Noah knew?"[29] we answer by asking, What was "the earth" that Adam and Eve knew when God told them, "Be fruitful, and multiply, and replenish *the earth,* and subdue it; and have dominion . . . over every living thing that moveth upon *the earth*" (Gen. 1:28)? Obviously, the true meaning of God's statements and commands cannot be limited by the ignorance of those who first heard Him speak!

Assuming, for the sake of argument, that the mountains were as high before the Flood as they are now (an assumption which characterizes the local Flood theory), then what are we to say of the idea that Noah's observation and information about geography was limited to the Mesopotamian valley? Even if he were a man of only average intelligence, he could have learned a great deal about the geography and topography of his own continent, Asia, where the highest mountains of the world are located, during the *six hundred years* that he lived before the Flood finally came. Assuming again, for the sake of argument, that Noah was the narrator of the entire Flood account (without the aid of supernatural revelation concerning the true magnitude of the Deluge), could he have been so ignorant of the topography of southwestern Asia as actually to think that the Flood covered *all the high mountains under the whole heaven* (Gen. 7:19), when it really covered only a few foothills?

Dr. Filby and others have denied that the expression "under the whole heaven" in Genesis 7:19 should be interpreted in an absolutely universal sense because there are other passages where it is not so used. For example, it must be used in a limited sense in Deuteronomy 2:25 ("the peoples that are under the whole heaven") because Moses goes on to limit it to "the peoples that are under the whole heaven, *who shall hear the report of thee."* In a parallel passage in Deuteronomy 11:25 Moses further limits this expression to mean *"all the land that ye shall tread upon."*[30]

29. Filby, *The Flood Reconsidered,* p. 81.
30. Filby, pp. 83, 98 (note No. 5). Derek Kidner points to other supposed examples of this "ancient sense" of understanding universal expressions in Colossians 1:23 and Acts 2:5 (*Genesis,* p. 94). Evangelical writers have gone to dangerous extremes in assuming that universal terms in Genesis 1-11 and such statements as "heaven above, the earth beneath, *and the water under the earth"* (Exod. 20:4) imply that Bible writers shared an antiquated world view with their pagan contemporaries (cf. Klaas Runia, *Karl Barth's*

But this is exactly the point which we have been emphasizing. When the context limits the meaning of universal terms, they must *not* be understood in the absolutely universal sense. When the context does not limit the meaning of such terms, they *almost certainly* are to be understood in the absolute sense. When the context *demands* a world-wide scope, as has been demonstrated to be the case in Genesis 6-9, a refusal to accept this fact simply indicates an attitude of unbelief at this point.

After discussing the ambiguity of such terms as "earth" *('eretz)* and "ground" *('adamāh),* Gleason L. Archer, Jr., concludes:

> But the phrase "under the whole heaven" in Gen. 7:19 may not be so easily disposed of. It is doubtful whether anywhere else in the Hebrew Scriptures this expression "the whole heaven" [in and of itself, apart from clear contextual evidence] can be interpreted to indicate a mere geographical region. For this reason most careful exegetes, like Franz Delitzsch in the last century and more recently H. C. Leupold, have not conceded the exegetical possibility of interpreting Genesis 7 as describing a merely local flood ... To suppose a 17,000-foot level in Armenia simultaneous with an uninundated Auvergne in France would be to propound a more incredible miracle than anything implied by the traditional understanding of a universal flood.[31]

Certainly one of the most serious charges to be laid at the door of the "limited observation and information" theory of the Flood is that it reduces the historical statements of Scripture to the level of mere fallible human opinion. The world view of Bible writers, we are told, must be understood from the standpoint of their "cultural environment," which is another way of saying that their statements are not always dependable. In discussing this and other subtle methods of undermining the clear statements of Scripture, Dr. J. Barton Payne comments:

> In recent conservatively-oriented publications, the princi-

Doctrine of Holy Scripture, Grand Rapids: Wm. B. Eerdmans Pub. Co., 1962, pp. 83-90). F. W. Grosheide and G. C. Aalders (whose views Runia rejects, p. 82) rightfully resisted such a trend. With regard to Exodus 20:4, it is surprising that Runia fails to note that Moses was speaking of *oceanic waters below the shoreline* (Deut. 4:18—"any fish that is in the waters beneath the earth"). See above, p. 34, note No. 30.

31. Gleason L. Archer, Jr., *A Survey of Old Testament Introduction* (Chicago: Moody Press, 1964), pp. 194-96.

ples of *usus loquendi,* normativeness, and progressive revelation seem to have shifted in function from that of an X-ray for exposing the meaning of Scripture to that of a cloak for avoiding it. In reference, for example, to the extent of the Flood, Bernard Ramm has concluded that when interpreted "phenomenally" and according to the cultural use of the narrator, the Deluge need be understood as covering only that part of the earth's surface as lay within the observation of the man who recorded it. But that the principle of *usus loquendi* is not the real basis for this interpretation is shown by Ramm's own summarization, as follows: "The flood is local, though spoken of in universal terms, and so the destruction of man is local though spoken of in universal terms." The account, in other words, conveys the thought of a universal catastrophe; but rational induction discountenances the possibility of a world-wide flood. It is, therefore, left to the rules of hermeneutics to gloss over the unacceptable words.[32]

It is significant that the neo-orthodox theologian Ralph H. Elliott appeals to Ramm's arguments as strong support for his own position that "the Flood was considered in universal terms because it was universal in its religious significance."[33] Thus, in typical neo-orthodox fashion, the early chapters of Genesis are lifted completely out of the realm of history and are transported into the realm of "Heilsgeschichte" or "religious myth."

Conclusion

By a truly remarkable array of evidences, the Bible sets forth the geographical universality of the Flood. The depth and duration of the Deluge, the need of a gigantic Ark to

---

32. J. Barton Payne, "Hermeneutics as a Cloak for the Denial of Scripture," *Bulletin of the Evangelical Theological Society,* Vol. 3, No. 4 (Fall, 1960), p. 94.

33. Ralph H. Elliott, *The Message of Genesis* (Nashville: Broadman Press, 1961), p. 67. In similar neo-orthodox fashion, Bernhard W. Anderson effectively evaporates the historicity of Genesis: "It is unnecessary to be concerned over the fact that archaeologists and geologists have found no evidence of a flood of such proportions that 'all the high mountains under the whole heaven were covered.' Through this story-form the narrator is dealing with something of far greater historical significance to him: the universality of human sin.... From the narrator's point of view, the universality of sin is matched by the universality of God's judgment. The flood must be total, complete." *The Beginnings of History,* ed. by William Barclay and F. F. Bruce (Nashville: Abingdon Press, 1963), pp. 53-54. See below, pp. 103 f.

enable terrestrial creatures to survive, the stated purpose of destroying a widely distributed human race, and the testimony of the apostle Peter establish beyond doubt the exegetical foundations for this doctrine of Scripture. The universal terms used in the Bible to describe this catastrophe require a world-wide Flood.

To be sure, many evangelical scholars continue to permit uniformitarian concepts of earth history to dominate their interpretation of Genesis 6-9.[34] However, it should also be noted that there is a significant number of scientists who *have* determined to allow the Word of God to be their guide in this vastly important area of investigation. The Creation Research Society, for example, which was organized in 1963, and which already claims several hundred members who hold advanced degrees in the natural sciences, places prominently in its Statement of Faith these words: "The great Flood described in Genesis, commonly referred to as the Noachian Flood, was an historic event, world-wide in its extent and effects."[35]

Our primary responsibility as faithful students of God's Word is not to manipulate and mold its statements into the framework of contemporary scientific theories; but rather to discover exactly what God has seen fit to reveal to us concerning the past history of this planet and its inhabitants. If this becomes our increasing passion and goal, we shall not be ultimately disappointed either as scientists or as theologians.

---

34. This fact has been clearly evidenced in the official publications of the American Scientific Affiliation. See below, pp. 105 ff.
35. For a brief survey of the history of the Creation Research Society, see Lammerts, *Why Not Creation?* pp. 1-4. A companion volume of selected articles from the C.R.S. quarterlies and annuals, also edited by Walter Lammerts, is entitled *Scientific Studies in Special Creation* (Nutley, N.J.: Presbyterian and Reformed Pub. Co., 1971). Another C.R.S. publication is *Biology: A Search for Order in Complexity,* ed. by John N. Moore and Harold S. Slusher (Grand Rapids: Zondervan Pub. House, 1970). Information concerning membership, dues, and the C.R.S. Quarterly may be obtained from Wilbert Rusch, Sr., 2717 Cranbrook Road, Ann Arbor, Michigan 48104.

3

the effects
of the flood
are visible today

APART FROM THE supernatural intervention of God, there could not have been a universal Flood in the days of Noah. By a miraculous display of God's power, the fountains of the great deep were broken up and the windows of heaven were opened. Additional miracles caused the sudden deepening of ocean basins and the corresponding uplift of continents and mountain ranges in order to bring an end to the Flood.

The Flood and Natural Processes

It is important to note, however, that not every aspect of the Flood was miraculous. For example, God did not create an ark for Noah. In harmony with the entire pattern of Scripture, material substances, natural processes, and human talents already available were used and directed by God for the accomplishment of His special purposes. Since Noah had the ability to construct an ark, given adequate instructions and time, God refused to make one for him, in spite of the fact that a created ark would doubtless have been perfect in form and therefore more comfortable for its occupants.

Similarly, the Lord Jesus Christ refused to employ the power of God to remove the huge stone from the entrance to Lazarus's tomb or even to loosen the grave clothes from his body. Those who stood by were perfectly able to accomplish such tasks. But the one thing they were absolutely helpless to accomplish, Jesus did accomplish, when he commanded Lazarus to come forth from the tomb. This pattern occurs so frequently in the Bible that we may almost state it as a principle: God refuses to do *miraculously* what man or natural processes can accomplish through His *providential direction.* God maintains a definite *economy of miracles.* Otherwise, miracles would become commonplace and would thus lose their uniqueness and significance.

Now when we apply this principle to the Flood itself, an interesting and important fact emerges. Apart from the specific miracles mentioned in Scripture, which were necessary to begin and to terminate this period of global judgment, the Flood accomplished its work of destruction *by purely natural processes* that are capable of being studied to a certain extent in hydraulics laboratories and in local flood situations today. In other words, when the stupendous masses of water which were released from the sky above and which were pushed up from the oceanic depths beneath began to move upon the continents, *they obeyed all the known laws of hydrodynamics.* There was nothing supernatural about the velocity and direction of movement or the erosional effect of the rushing waters. If there had been, Scripture would so indicate. Just as the waters of the Jordan, piled up near Zarethan, "returned unto their place, and went over all its banks, as aforetime" (Josh. 4:18) when they were supernaturally released, so also in Noah's day gravity and other natural forces, acting upon the masses of water that were supernaturally released, moved them back and forth across the earth during the year of the Deluge.

This principle is important, for there have always been those who would seek to solve the conflict between Genesis and uniformitarian geology by multiplying the miracles of the Flood. To keep the Flood local in extent and thus "scientifically reasonable," it has been suggested that the mountains of the Near East sank below sea level within forty days so the Flood could cover those mountains and yet not affect the rest of the earth.[1] A similar plan would be to cover these mountains with water, but confine the Flood to this one region by means of a huge invisible wall. Or, if the Flood was actually universal, perhaps God made it so gentle and tranquil in its movements that it neither disturbed the topography of the earth nor destroyed the trees![2]

Such theories are indeed spectacular for their ingenuity and for the way in which they neatly "harmonize" the Genesis of Moses with the geology of Lyell;[3] but they are totally unbiblical. When the Scriptures inform us that the Flood covered "all the high mountains that were *under the whole heaven,*" and that all living things were destroyed "with the earth" (Gen. 6:13), *we must be prepared to find world-wide geologic effects of this aqueous catastrophe.*

The Destructive Power of Moving Water

Since the days of Noah, men have had an awesome fear of floods. Nothing can quite compare to the terror and sense of helplessness that people experience when in the presence

---

1. Cf. Ramm, *The Christian View,* pp. 238-39.
2. Cf. Whitcomb and Morris, *The Genesis Flood,* pp. 97-106, for an analysis of the "tranquil theory" and the problem of the olive leaf episode in Genesis 8:6-12 which constitutes the supposed Biblical basis for this theory.
3. Even as Thomas Aquinas "harmonized" Scripture with Aristotle— a merger from which Roman Catholic theology has never yet recovered. Cf. Colin Brown, *Philosophy and the Christian Faith* (Chicago: Inter-Varsity Press, 1969), p. 25.

of huge masses of water on the rampage. Our nation will never forget what happened to Johnstown, Pennsylvania, in 1889, when 20,000,000 tons of water from Conemaugh Lake swept into the city and killed 2,200 people.[4] The Ohio and Mississippi River floods of 1937 killed 400, left 1,000,000 homeless, and destroyed $500,000,000 worth of property. In South America, in May of 1970, an avalanche of water, rocks, and mud, rushing nearly 100 miles an hour down the slopes of the Andes, totally buried the Peruvian cities of Yungay and Ranrahirca with 14,000 inhabitants.[5] Six months later, on the other side of the world, "a ghastly 25-foot high wave driven by winds of from 100 to 150 miles an hour rolled in from the Bay of Bengal to annihilate the over-crowded lowlands of the Ganges-Brahmaputra River Delta in the dead of night. The death and destruction rank with the worst the world has known. Whole islands were inundated. Families and villages were instantly wiped out by the wall of water.... The most reliable estimates put the number of dead at *half a million,* but the toll could reach a million. And throughout a 3,000 square mile area, 3,500,000 were left homeless."[6]

Modern river floods have been known to carry boulders weighing hundreds of tons for great distances in a matter of hours and to excavate deep gorges and to sweep away entire forests. A single brief flood in the San Gabriel Mountains near Los Angeles eroded and redeposited up to 100,000 cubic yards of debris from each square mile of the watershed.[7] "At Cherbourg, France, a breakwater was composed of large rocks and capped with a wall ·20 feet high. Storm waves hurled 7,000 pound stones over the wall and moved 65-ton concrete blocks 60 feet."[8]

Now if local floods can accomplish such destruction in our modern world, what may be said of a flood so gigantic that *it rose above the very highest mountains and swept over the entire earth for twenty-two weeks before it even*

4. Cf. David G. McCullough, *The Johnstown Flood* (New York: Simon and Schuster, Inc., 1968).
5. Charles Lekberg, "The Killer Among Us," in *The 1971 World Book Year Book* (Chicago: Field Enterprises Educational Corp., 1971), p. 294. See also Gordon Gaskill's description of the 1963 flood at Longarone, Italy, which took over 2,000 lives in six minutes: "The Night the Mountain Fell," *Reader's Digest,* May, 1965, pp. 59-67.
6. Lekberg, "The Killer Among Us," p. 294.
7. Cf. Whitcomb and Morris, *The Genesis Flood,* p. 263.
8. Willard Bascom, "Ocean Waves," *Scientific American,* August, 1959, pp. 80-83.

THE DESTRUCTIVE POWER OF RIVER FLOODS

"The astonishing power exerted by a flood of rushing water, both in scouring and in transporting material, is rarely fully appreciated even today" (Cyril S. Fox, *Water,* New York, Philosophical Library, 1953, p. xiv). Rivers in flood stage normally excavate their beds to tremendous depths, carrying vast quantities of sediment along in suspension or along the bed, to be redeposited downstream when the flood subsides.

"When the Colorado River was in flood it was acting on the solid rock of its bed down to a depth of over 120 feet from the top of the flood water . . . it could flush with great force more than 115 feet of sand-filled cuttings. Without such proofs few engineers would be inclined to believe that silting follows sand movements down to depths of 50 and 100 feet below normal bed level at each time of high flood" (*ibid.*, p. 111).

If this kind of activity occurs during present-day localized floods, what must have been the tremendous quantities of sediment eroded and transported *when rain poured forth over all the earth for at least forty days without stopping, and the fountains of the great deep were broken up continuously for five months!* (See Whitcomb and Morris, *The Genesis Flood,* pp. 259-61).

began to subside? Obviously, every movable object would have been swept away and the crust of the earth would never be the same again. An acceptance of the authority and historicity of the Biblical record plus a recognition of the stupendous power of rushing masses of water makes it impossible to take seriously any "tranquil theory" of the Flood! Either the Book of Genesis with its supernatural global catastrophism, or uniformitarian geology with its essential tranquilism, must set the pattern for our thinking with regard to earth history, for both views cannot be accepted simultaneously in a rational universe.[9]

It is not surprising, therefore, that Sir Charles Lyell (1799-1873), whom Darwin called "the head of the uniformitarians," was desperately opposed to the Book of Genesis. He hoped he could drive men "out of the Mosaic record." The Mosaic Deluge, especially, he claimed, had been "an incubus to the science of geology."[10] Charles Lyell was a theist and, like him, many other scientists who call themselves Christians have been unhappy about the early chapters of Genesis. This is indeed tragic, for the Lord Jesus Christ emphasized the divine authority of the first book of the Bible and quoted repeatedly from its early chapters as factual history (Matt. 19:4; Luke 17:29, 32). In fact, He referred specifically to the Flood as a supernatural judgment which destroyed all men outside of the Ark and used this as an analogy for the final judgment of the world (Matt. 24:39; Luke 17:26-30). *How can one claim to be a Christian and at the same time question the statements of the Lord Jesus Christ?*

The Stratigraphic Effects of the Flood

Those who deny that there is any geologic evidence of a universal Flood apparently do not know what the effects of such a flood would be. If we persuade ourselves that a world-wide flood would produce chaotic heaps of mixed materials of all sizes and shapes, scattered here and there across the earth, then it is not surprising that we find no evidences of the Genesis Flood! Hydraulic engineers, who devote their professional lives to the study of water action, ought to be our authorities on this subject, rather than historical and

---

9. Cf. R. Hooykaas, *The Principle of Uniformity in Geology, Biology, and Theology,* pp. 1-66.
10. *Life, Letters, and Journals of Sir Charles Lyell,* I, 253, 256, 328; quoted in Robert T. Clark and James D. Bales, *Why Scientists Accept Evolution* (Nutley, N.J.: Presbyterian and Reformed Pub. Co., 1966), p. 19.

descriptive geologists. And yet, as is too often true in the world of science today, specialists in one field remain comparatively ignorant of the principles that underlie a cognate branch of science. In the words of Dr. J. Oliver Buswell, Jr., "One of the besetting sins of scientists is the ignoring of related fields of study."[11]

Henry M. Morris, who received his Ph.D. from the University of Minnesota (1950) in hydrology and hydraulics, with minors in geology and mathematics, served three years as a hydrological engineer with the United States government and has spent twenty-nine years in university teaching and research. From 1957 to 1970 he was Professor of Hydraulic Engineering and Chairman of the Department of Civil Engineering at the Virginia Polytechnic Institute and State University. Dr. Morris has gained an international reputation for his textbook on *Applied Hydraulics in Engineering,* (2nd ed. co-authored with James M. Wiggert; New York: Ronald Press Co., 1972; 629 pp.) and for his numerous technical articles in this field. The writer wishes to take this opportunity to thank Dr. Morris for his generosity in sharing his vast experience in the principles of hydraulic engineering as they apply to the Biblical account of the Flood.

Dr. Morris has pointed out that according to the law of hydrodynamic selectivity a flood of the magnitude described in Genesis, with its unbelievably vast complex of sediment-saturated currents, would of necessity produce horizontal, superimposed layers of materials, selected by the moving waters according to their specific gravity and sphericity.[12] As each current of water slowed down and deposited its load, another current would come from perhaps a different direction, carrying somewhat different types of materials, depositing them on top of the first layer without disturbing it. Thus, as various currents moved across the earth during the months of the Flood, a great series of sedimentary strata would be formed in various parts of the earth, in some cases to depths of many thousands of feet.[13]

---

11. J. Oliver Buswell, Jr., Letter to the Editor, *JASA,* December, 1963, p. 122.
12. Whitcomb and Morris, *The Genesis Flood,* p. 274. See also Henry M. Morris, "Sedimentation and the Fossil Record: A Study in Hydraulic Engineering," in *Why Not Creation?* (Walter Lammerts, ed.), pp. 125-27, 133-35.
13. Whitcomb and Morris, *The Genesis Flood,* p. 147. In addition to currents, there must have been an enormous complexity of great "tidal waves" (tsunamis) during the Flood year. Joseph Bernstein points out that "in the deep waters of the Pacific these waves reach

One of the most spectacular evidences of what a year-long, world-wide Flood would accomplish may be seen in the Grand Canyon of Arizona. This gigantic formation is in some places more than 5,000 feet deep, 25,000 feet across, and extends for more than 100 miles to the east and west. As far as the eye can see, thick, horizontal deposits of various types of sediments rest conformably upon one another from the bottom of the canyon to the top.

According to uniformitarian concepts, numerous changes in environment, with great regional subsidences and uplifts, must have been involved, each layer representing millions of years of river deposits in a vast geosyncline or shallow sea, which gradually sank as the deposits accumulated. But this would be quite inconceivable. The strata simply could not have remained so nearly uniform and horizontal over such great areas and great periods of time, while undergoing such repeated and vast movements. "A better explanation according to creationists is that it was formed rapidly as water cut through not yet consolidated material that had been deposited by the flood of Noah's time. This explanation is superior because it conforms to *the principles of hydrodynamics*. These principles state that water can not meander at the same time that it is cutting a deeper channel. The channel of the Colorado River is both deep and meandering."[14]

Dr. Clifford Burdick, a geologist who has devoted a number of years to the study of the Grand Canyon formations, explains some of the insurmountable problems that confront the standard uniformitarian interpretation of these rocks:

Below the Mississippian in most places the Devonian is not

---

a speed of 500 miles an hour." But contrary to popular opinion, "tsunamis are so shallow in comparison with their length that in in the open ocean they are hardly detectable. Their amplitude sometimes is as little as two feet from trough to crest. Usually it is only when they approach shallow water or the shore that they build up to their terrifying heights" ("Tsunamis," *Scientific American*, August, 1954, p. 61). Such "tidal waves" would thus have had very little effect on Noah's Ark. Jack Durkee's widely-read description of the universal Flood view as involving "tidal waves rushing at thousands of miles an hour" must be labeled a caricature (*Who Says?* ed. by Fritz Ridenour; Glendale, Calif.: Gospel Light Publications, 1967, p. 147).

14. Moore and Slusher, editors, *Biology: A Search for Order in Complexity* (Grand Rapids: Zondervan Pub. House, 1970), p. 412. See also Morris and Wiggert, *Applied Hydraulics in Engineering,* 2nd ed. (New York: Ronald Press Co., 1972), p. 523; and Whitcomb Morris, *The Genesis Flood,* pp. 152-55, for photographs and explanations of these formations.

THE GRAND CANYON

Spectacular exposures of flat-lying sedimentary rocks such as those in the Grand Canyon provide ample visible evidence of Deluge deposition. In this area, there are thousands of square miles of horizontal strata, thousands of feet thick, supposed to have been deposited over about half a billion years! The strata include limestones, shales, and sandstones. According to uniformist concepts, numerous changes of environment, with great regional subsidences and uplifts, must have been involved, but this would appear quite impossible. The strata simply could *not* have remained so nearly uniform and horizontal over such great areas and great periods of time, while undergoing such repeated epeirogenic movements. By far the most reasonable way of accounting for them is in terms of relatively rapid deposition out of the sediment-laden water of the Flood. Following the Flood, while the rocks were still comparatively soft and unconsolidated, the great canyons were rapidly scoured out as the waters rushed down from the newly uplifted peneplains to the newly enlarged ocean basins. (See Whitcomb and Morris, *The Genesis Flood,* pp. 151-54).

The recent discovery of "spores of plants at least closely related to pines in the pre-Cambrian" strata of the Grand Canyon "makes it extremely difficult to visualize any evolutionary development of these specialized plants. The undoubted occurrence of pollen of flowering plants is even more difficult to explain in usually accepted evolutionary concepts" (Clifford L. Burdick, "Microflora of the Grand Canyon," *Creation Research Society Quarterly,* May, 1966, p. 50). See also Clifford L. Burdick, "Progress Report on Grand Canyon Palynology," *Creation Research Society Quarterly,* June, 1972, pp. 25-30.

present and nowhere does the Silurian or the Ordovician appear, which means that the Redwall formation which is Lower Mississippian actually rests upon the Cambrian Muav limestone, a time gap of over 50,000,000 years. Surely in this immense space of time we would expect to find effects of very extensive erosion, perhaps warping and folding with angular discordance, but what do we actually find? The appearance of a perfectly conformable series of beds, laid down in fairly quick succession. Surely there is cause for astonishment![15]

These flat-lying sedimentary rocks, exposed to view in the Grand Canyon and many other spectacular canyons, cover an area of a quarter of a million square miles, including most of Utah and Arizona and large segments of Colorado and New Mexico. According to Dr. Burdick and others who have studied such formations, the only adequate explanation is a vast complex of rapidly-moving currents of water of worldwide scope.

The Formation of Fossil Beds

Not only do sedimentary deposits demand the dynamics of a gigantic flood for adequate explanation, but so also do the fossils of billions of plants and animals that are found within them. This is indeed a serious problem for evolutionary uniformitarianism, for large-scale fossilization is simply *not* occurring anywhere in the world today. When fishes die in the oceans they do not sink to the bottom and become fossils. Instead, they either decompose or are picked to pieces by scavengers. Likewise, as one prominent geologist has pointed out, "The buffalo carcasses strewn over the plains in uncounted millions two generations ago have left hardly a present trace. The flesh was devoured by wolves or vultures within hours or days after death, and even the skeletons have now largely disappeared, the bones dissolving and crumbling into dust under the attack of weather."[16] The Old Testament indicates that Palestine was infested with lions for centuries (Job 38:39, Prov. 22:13, II Kings 17:25), but no fossil of a lion has yet been found there.[17]

15. Clifford L. Burdick, "Streamlining Stratigraphy," in *Scientific Studies in Special Creation,* ed. by Walter Lammerts (Nutley, N.J.: Presbyterian and Reformed Pub. Co., 1971), pp. 127-28. See also, in the same volume, Harold W. Clark, "The Mystery of the Red Beds," pp. 156-64.
16. Carl O. Dunbar, *Historical Geology* (New York: Wiley & Sons, 1949), p. 39.
17. Personal communication from Dr. Nelson Glueck, April 20, 1959.

In contrast to this lack of fossilization going on in the world today, consider the almost unbelievable amount of fossilization that has occurred in the past. "It has been estimated that more than 100,000 different species of fossils have already been found. Some rocks are composed almost entirely of the remains of marine animals."[18] Nothing could be more obvious than the fact that billions of fossils of crustaceans, fishes, land animals, and plants, many of them almost perfectly preserved in huge sedimentary deposits, could not have been buried by processes observable in the world today.

A startling illustration of the fact that a great catastrophe once struck this planet may be found in the four or five million mammoths and other large animals which were destroyed in the north polar regions, many of them frozen instantly and preserved whole and undamaged, and in some cases either standing or kneeling upright!

Ivan T. Sanderson, a prominent field zoologist who spent many years studying these phenomena, had attempted at first to explain the mass destruction of Arctic mammoths in non-catastrophic terms.[19] But a special study of the Beresovka mammoth, which Russian scientists had transported from Siberia to the Leningrad Museum, caused his position to be "almost completely reversed."

> First, the mammoth was upright, but it had a broken hip. Second, its exterior was whole and perfect, with none of its two-foot long shaggy fur rubbed or torn off. Third, it was fresh; its parts, although they started to rot when the heat of fire got at them, were just as they had been in life; the stomach contents had not begun to decompose. Finally, there were buttercups on its tongue.[20]

Animals as large as mammoths would require several hundred pounds of food daily just to survive; and there were many millions of them in this region where very little vegetation grows today. In order to freeze animals of this size in such a way that large crystals would not form within their body cells, temperatures of 150 degrees below zero would have to descend upon them instantly. Such conditions

18. International Christian Crusade, *Evolution: Science Falsely So-called,* 18th ed. (205 Yonge St., Rm. 31, Toronto 1; 1970), p. 17.
19. Ivan T. Sanderson, "The Riddle of the Mammoths," *Saturday Evening Post* (Dec. 7, 1946), pp. 127, 142, 144, 147.
20. Ivan T. Sanderson, "Riddle of the Frozen Giants," *Saturday Evening Post* (Jan. 16, 1960), p. 82.

MAMMOTHS

An estimated 5,000,000 mammoths, whose remains are buried all along the coastline of northern Siberia and Alaska, were frozen and buried not many thousands of years ago. "The Siberian deposits have been worked now for nearly two centuries. The store appears to be as inexhaustible as a coalfield. Some think that a day may come when the spread of civilization may cause the utter disappearance of the elephant in Africa, and that it will be to these deposits that we may have to turn as the only source of animal ivory" ("Ivory," *Encyclopedia Britannica,* 1956, XII, 834).

"One mine in Siberia reportedly yielded twenty thousand tusks. When Vitus Bering, the Danish explorer of the Arctic, visited Bear Island, north of Siberia in the Artic Ocean, ;ie reported it was composed of two ingredients, mammoth remains and sand. But the predominant ingredient was mammoth bones. During the eighteenth and nineteenth centuries, reports occasionally came in of mammoths found in frozen state. Some of these reports were investigated by the Tsarist governments, and a few mammoths were exhumed and brought to St. Petersburg. They were rather sensational evidences of the time when Siberia had had a much more temperate or subtropical climate. When Baron Toll explored Bennet Island, some three hundred miles north of the Siberian mainland, he reported finding a quick-frozen mammoth, in a land where today, during the height of the Arctic summer, willows will grow perhaps two inches high. . . . And yet here, Baron Toll found evidence of former life under conditions which today could not possibly exist. Concerning mammoth bones in Russia, Pallas claimed

that there was not a river bed in all Russia, from the Don to the Bering Strait, which did not contain mammoth bones. Other writers have observed that, strangely enough, the farther one goes north, the more numerous are mammoth remains" (Donald W. Patten, "The Ice Epoch," in *A Symposium on Creation,* by Henry M. Morris and others; Grand Rapids: Baker Book House, 1968, p. 128).

The fact that only a catastrophe of the proportions described in Genesis 6-9 could have suddenly destroyed these vast numbers of large animals is becoming more and more obvious to unprejudiced investigators.

could very well have existed in various places within the higher latitudes at the early stages of the collapse of the antediluvian vapor canopy (Gen. 7:11).[21] One thing is certain—all uniformitarian interpretations have failed dismally. "Lyell knew about the mammoths and saw that they endangered his theory. He tried to explain them away, suggesting they were caught in a cold snap while swimming; which does not tally with the facts. Darwin also knew the story, and confessed that he saw no solution to it."[22]

In Lincoln County, Wyoming, almost perfect specimens of fish, turtles, insects, and mammals have been found together with huge palm leaves, from 6 to 8 feet in length and from 3 to 4 feet wide.[23] Even more significantly, trillions of tons of vegetation, much of it perfectly preserved, even to leaves and flowers, have been buried in all parts of the world, including Antarctica,[24] in the form of coal. Each foot of coal represents many feet of compressed plant remains, and some coal seams are as much as thirty or forty feet in thickness. Obviously, no such process of coal formation is going on today, and the so-called "peat-bog theory" is a poor attempt to cope with this problem. As Morris explains:

> The Dismal Swamp of Virginia, perhaps the most frequently cited case of a potential coal bed, has formed only an average of 7 feet of peat, hardly enough to make a single respectable seam of coal. Furthermore, there is no actual evidence that peat is now being transformed into coal anywhere in the world. No locality is known where the peat bed, in its lower reaches, grades into a typical coal bed. All known coal beds, therefore, seem to have been formed in the past and are not continuing to be formed in the present, as the principle of uniformity could reasonably be expected to imply.[25]

---

21. Cf. Whitcomb and Morris, *The Genesis Flood,* pp. 288-303.
22. Norman Macbeth, *Darwin Retried* (Boston: Gambit, Inc., 1971), p. 115.
23. "Fishing for Fossils," *Compressed Air Magazine* Vol. 63 (March, 1958), p. 24.
24. See *National Geographic Magazine,* Feb., 1963, pp. 288 (photo), 296.
25. Whitcomb and Morris, *The Genesis Flood,* p. 164. See also Harold G. Coffin, "Research on the Classic Joggins Petrified Trees," in the *Creation Research Society Quarterly* (June, 1969), pp. 35-44; and "A Paleoecological Misinterpretation," *CRSQ* (Sept. 1968), pp. 85-87. The latter article has been reprinted in *Scientific Studies in Special Creation,* ed. by Walter Lammerts (Nutley, N.J.: Presbyterian and Reformed Pub. Co., 1971), pp. 165 ff.

In the volume titled *Why Not Creation?* may be seen a remarkable photograph of a large tree trunk turned into coal, penetrating vertically through several layers of sedimentary strata.[26] Surely this constitutes the final blow to the uniformist theory of coal formation, for no tree could have remained in an upright position for thousands of years while sediments built up around it!

Another remarkable discovery is the perfectly preserved tracks of many kinds of animals, including dinosaurs.[27] Among these dinosaur tracks have been found the footprints of human beings of great stature.[28] Also, such ordinarily ephemeral imprints as ripple marks and raindrop splash marks have been discovered quite frequently. These simply could not have been preserved apart from unique sedimentation processes.[29]

Catastrophic Phenomena in Geology

Although sedimentary and fossil formations may be the most obvious evidences that huge masses of water once swept across this planet, there are other features of the earth's crust that defy explanation on any other basis. In discussing the mechanisms that must have been employed in forming the lowest levels of the geologic column, Walter S. Olson, by no means a Biblical catastrophist, observes:

> The erosive power and heating effect of such [global] tides can account for all the phenomena associated with the Infra-Cambrian deposits. ... The tides would eventually sweep across the interior and, laden with sediment and rock fragments, abrade the land surface and reduce the continents to peneplains. ... The tidal friction would raise the ocean temperatures to unprecedented levels, bringing carbon dioxide out of solution to precipitate calcium carbonate .... Ancient mountain systems were worn down to their roots ... leaving a clean slate on which the record came to be written which is usually called historical geology.[30]

When the continents arose from the waters of the Flood, the

---

26. N. A. Rupke, "Prolegomena to a Study of Cataclysmal Sedimentation," in *Why Not Creation?*, p. 153.
27. Cf. Roland T. Bird, "We Captured a 'Live' Brontosaur," *National Geographic Magazine,* May, 1954, pp. 707-22.
28. Cf. A. E. Wilder Smith, *Man's Origin, Man's Destiny* (Wheaton, Ill.: Harold Shaw Pub., 1968), pp. 96-97, 293-98.
29. Cf. Rupke, "Prolegomena," photographs, pp. 165-71.
30. Walter S. Olson, "Origin of the Cambrian-Precambrian Unconformity," *American Scientist,* LIV, No. 4 (December, 1966), pp. 461-62, 458.

THE COASTLINE OF ANTARCTICA

The frozen and forbidding shoreline of the South Polar continent challenges our imagination as to its former condition. The fact that it was once warm and humid and had abundant vegetation is shown by "widespread discoveries of coal and petrified wood" (*National Geographic Magazine*, Feb., 1963, pp. 288, 296; cf. Nov., 1971, p. 653).

GREAT COAL DEPOSITS

Enormous masses of vegetation that existed all over the world just before the Flood were swept into huge piles here and there, repeatedly covered with layers of mud, and carbonized through heat caused by enormous thrust and weight pressures. "The formation of coal from woody or other cellulosic material in a very short time was demonstrated by experiments performed by Dr. George R. Hill of the College of Mines and Mineral Industries of the University of Utah. His report may be found in *Chem Tech*, May, 1972, p. 296. . . . The significance of these results with reference to the Flood and other catastrophic models is evident from Dr. Hill's remarks. He stated that, 'These observations suggest that in their formation, high rank coals, i.e., anthracite and low volatile bituminous, . . . were probably subjected to high temperature at some stage in their history. *A possible mechanism for formation of these high rank coals could have been a short time, rapid heating event.*'" (Duane T. Gish, *Acts and Facts,* Vol. 1, No. 4, Institute for Creation Research, 2716 Madison Ave., San Diego, Calif. 92116). See also Melvin Cook, *Prehistory and Earth Models* (London: Max Parrish & Co., Ltd., 1966), pp. 235-37.

outwash formed vast fluviatile plains or alluvial slopes such as the one that stretches from the Rockies to the Mississippi and from Canada to Mexico.[31]

Enclosed lake basins such as Bonneville in Utah, Lahonton in Nevada, and Tahoe in California were once filled with water.[32] Raised river terraces reaching from the Atlantic to the present Mississippi show that rivers once carried much larger volumes of water than do their present remnants.[33] Also, such phenomena as the incised, or entrenched, meanders, where strong lateral cutting of rivers took place simultaneously with down-cutting, can only be explained on the basis that the horizontal beds were still soft and unconsolidated soon after deposition during the Flood period, when most of the meander formation took place.[34]

Huge mountain ranges give every evidence of sudden and comparatively recent upthrust; and yet, in the words of Dr. A. J. Eardley, "the cause of the deformation of the earth's outer layers and the consequent building of mountains still effectively evades an explanation."[35] As Morris observes, uniformitarianism cannot account for the origin of geosynclines, the continued subsidence necessary to accumulate thousands of feet of sediments, the source areas from which these great volumes of sediments must have eroded, and the uplift and deformation of these geosynclines to form the present mountain ranges. Nor can it explain the existence of great peneplains, dry canyons or coulees, hanging valleys, dry waterfalls, and rock-rimmed basins.[36]

The presence of enormous masses of igneous (volcanic) rock all over the world is another problem for uniformitarianism. Often they are found intruding into previously deposited sedimentary rocks or on the surface covering vast areas of earlier deposits. The Columbia Plateau, of the northwestern United States, is a tremendous lava plateau of almost incredible thickness (several thousand feet) covering

31. N. M. Fenneman, *Physiography of Western United States* (New York: McGraw-Hill Pub. Co., 1931), pp. 11, 14, 147, 274.
32. Walter E. Lammerts, "On the Recent Origin of the Pacific Southwest Deserts," *C.R.S. Quarterly*, June, 1971, pp. 50-54.
33. Whitcomb and Morris, *The Genesis Flood*, p. 318. See also the remarkable demonstration of the recent origin of the Mississippi delta by Benjamin F. Allen, "The Geologic Age of the Mississippi River," *Creation Research Society Quarterly*, Sept., 1972, pp. 96-114.
34. Whitcomb and Morris, *The Genesis Flood*, pp. 153-55.
35. A. J. Eardley, "The Cause of Mountain Building—An Enigma," *American Scientist*, June, 1957, p. 189.
36. Whitcomb and Morris, *The Genesis Flood*, pp. 147-49.

about 200,000 square miles. But the only modern process at all pertinent to these phenomena is that of volcanism, which in its present character could not possibly have produced these great igneous formations. There are perhaps five hundred active volcanoes in the world, and possibly three times that many extinct volcanoes. But nothing ever seen by man in the present era can compare with whatever the phenomena were which caused the formation of these tremendous structures. The principle of uniformity breaks down completely at this important point of geologic interpretation. Some manifestation of catastrophic action alone (such as the breaking up of the fountains of the great deep during the Flood) is sufficient.[37]

Apart from the catastrophe of the Flood, with its accompanying collapse of the great vapor canopy, there has yet to be devised a scheme that even comes near to explaining the origin of continental ice sheets. W. D. Thornbury points out that "some 4,000,000 square miles of North America, 2,000,000 squares miles or more of Europe, and an as yet little known but possibly comparable area in Siberia were glaciated. In addition, many lesser areas were covered by local ice caps. Thousands of valley glaciers existed in mountains where today there are either no glaciers or only small ones."[38]

Dr. William L. Stokes of the University of Utah admits that "the underlying cause of glaciation remains in doubt. ... At least 29 'explanations' have been advanced to account for widespread glaciations. Most of these had little chance of survival from the first, but others enjoyed some degree of success until they were rendered untenable by subsequently accumulated information."[39]

The end of the ice age is much more recent than was once speculated, and there is much evidence now available that there was only one great glaciation, not four.[40] This indicates that the time is ripe for a completely fresh and unbiased study of the pre-Flood vapor canopy concept and of the possible effects of its sudden collapse.

Yet another example of the failure of the uniformity prin-

---

37. Whitcomb and Morris, *The Genesis Flood,* pp. 138-39.
38. Wm. D. Thornbury, *Principles of Geomorphology* (New York: Wiley & Sons, 1954), p. 354.
39. Wm. L. Stokes, "Another Look at the Ice Age," *Science,* Oct. 28, 1955, p. 815.
40. Cf. Wm. A. Springstead, "Monoglaciology and the Global Flood," *Creation Research Society Quarterly,* Dec., 1971, pp. 175 ff.; and Whitcomb and Morris, *The Genesis Flood,* pp. 296-303.

EXPLODING MOUNTAINS SINCE THE FLOOD

About 4600 B.C., the 12,000-foot Mount Mazama exploded and flung *seventeen cubic miles of rock* into the air, resulting in a loss of over 5,000 feet of its height. Then the core collapsed and water filled it (to form Crater Lake) to the present enormous depth of 1,932 feet, surrounded by rims from 500 to 2,000 feet high (cf. *National Geographic Magazine,* July, 1962, p. 128).

About 1520 B.C., the Aegean volcanic isle of Thera exploded, causing 32 square miles of the island to sink into the sea to a depth of 1,300 feet in places, snuffing out the brilliant Minoan civilization there and on nearby Crete (cf. Spyridon Marinatos, "Thera: Key to the Riddle of Minos," *National Geographic Magazine,* May, 1972, pp. 702-26).

In August of 1883, the island of Krakatoa in the Netherlands East Indies (now Indonesia) "burst with a roar heard more than 2,000 miles away; the resultant aerial vibra-

tions circled the globe several times. . . . Volcanic dust blocked out the sun for a radius of 100 miles. Some of it eventually sifted to earth 1,000 miles from Krakatoa; the rest, ejected with a force that drove it into the stratosphere, dispersed over the entire planet, causing specticular sunsets through the closing months of 1883. Finally came the culminating horror—the tidal waves. More than 100 feet high and with a velocity in excess of 50 miles an hour, they ravaged the nearby coasts of Java and Sumatra. In places they raged inland of 1,000 yards and were still 30 feet high. They swept away entire towns and villages, almost 300 of them. This disaster crushed the life from more than 36,000 people" (*ibid.,* p. 715).

Multiply these crustal paroxysms by hundreds of thousands and a mental picture of the early phase of the Flood year will begin to emerge—"on the same day were all the fountains of the great deep broken up . . . and every living thing was destroyed" (Gen. 7:11, 23).

ciple to account for significant features of the earth's crust is the "thrust-fault" hypothesis, as applied to such areas as the Heart Mountain Thrust of Wyoming and the Lewis Overthrust of Montana and Alberta. The latter formation, which includes the Glacier National Park area, is 350 miles wide, and has an inferred horizontal displacement of at least 35 or 40 miles, in spite of the fact that the supposed fault plane dips at an angle of only 3 degrees. The black rocks on the upper half of the mountain are Pre-Cambrian, while the lighter-colored rocks below are Cretaceous, at least 500,000,000 years younger, according to the uniformitarian scheme of dating fossils! Of course, no uniformist can allow for such a colossal exception to his timetable, for this would be equivalent to assuming that in this part of the world dinosaurs evolved into crab-like trilobites! Therefore, evolutionists believe that the Pre-Cambrian rocks must have pushed thirty-five or forty miles over on top of the Cretaceous shales!

Among evangelical scientists, Frank H. Roberts[41] and J. R. van de Fliert[42] have claimed that the evidence of much folding and faulting in these areas proves that the uniformist view is basically correct. However, these small-scale disturbances in the rocks are nothing compared to the magnitude of the Lewis "overthrust" concept, for which there is no real evidence. Furthermore, and more important, it is quite inconceivable that sufficient force could be generated in the earth's crust to move *eight hundred thousand billion tons of rocks* with both a vertical and lateral component (against the force of gravity and the frictional force along the sliding plane). Dr. Henry Morris has demonstrated that on the basis of known friction coefficients for sliding blocks, so much shearing stress would be developed in a large block that the material itself would fail in compression and, therefore, could not transported as a coherent block at all.[43] M. K. Hubbert and W. W. Rubey concede that this would be a "mechanical impossibility."[44]

41. Frank H. Roberts, Review of *The Genesis Flood,* in *JASA,* March, 1964, p. 29.
42. J. R. van de Fliert, "Fundamentalism and the Fundamentals of Geology," *JASA,* September, 1969, pp. 75-77.
43. Whitcomb and Morris, *The Genesis Flood,* p. 191.
44. M. K. Hubbert and W. W. Rubey, "Role of Fluid Pressure in Mechanics of Overthrust Faulting," *Bulletin of Geological Society of America,* Feb., 1959, pp. 122, 126. For more recent studies of "overthrusts," see the following articles in the *Creation Research Society Quarterly:* Harold S. Slusher, "Supposed Overthrust in Franklin Mountains, El Paso, Texas," May, 1966; Walter E. Lam-

We must, therefore, conclude that in this area "Pre-Cambrian" rocks were deposited after "Cretaceous" rocks, and thus the widely accepted uniformitarian timetable of earth history is largely meaningless. Seen from the standpoint of the Biblical doctrine of the Flood, such formations simply indicate that burial patterns in some parts of the world did not follow the normal ecological zonation of creatures. In other words, sea creatures would normally be buried deeper in any given sequence, but in the complexity of Deluge hydrodynamics many exceptions could be anticipated.

Conclusion

If the universal Flood concept explains far better than other concepts many of the significant features of the earth's crust, why is it not more generally accepted by geologists? The answer, we feel, is twofold. In the first place, nothing less than a supernatural intervention could have caused such a Flood; and modern science, in the nature of the case, has no room whatsoever for such interventions. In the second place, the vast majority of historical geologists have never even studied the relative merits of the uniformist approach as over against global catastrophism and, therefore, can hardly qualify as competent and impartial judges in the matter.

Consider, for example, this statement by C. P. Martin of McGill University concerning the theory of evolution:

> By far the greater number of students that come my way—and they are drawn from many American and Canadian universities—are completely indoctrinated with the idea that the theory of evolution by mutation is a closed issue, an unquestionable established fact. It is not that they are aware of the difficulties which I have mentioned above and esteem them of little weight or importance; they never heard of them and are amazed at the bare possibility of the accepted theory being criticized.[45]

---

merts, "Overthrust Faults in Glacier National Park," May, 1966; Clifford L. Burdick and Harold Slusher, "The Empire Mountains—A Thrust Fault?" June, 1969; Clifford L. Burdick, "The Lewis Overthrust," September, 1969; Walter E. Lammerts, "The Glarus Overthrust," March, 1972; and George F. Howe, "Overthrust Evidence as Observed at Faults Caused by the San Fernando Earthquake," March, 1972.

45. C. P. Martin, "A Nongeneticist Looks at Evolution," *American Scientist,* January, 1953, p. 105. For a more recent and very similar statement, see G. A. Kerkut, *Implications of Evolution* (New York: Pergamon Press, 1960), pp. 3-5.

A VOLCANO IS BORN

The birthday of the great Parícutin volcano was February 20, 1943. A cornfield 180 miles west of Mexico City "suddenly began to produce a dense cloud of smoke. By the second day a cinder cone had reached an altitude of 100 feet. Showers of rock and fragments of gas-filled lava burst from the new volcano's throat with each rumbling explosion. They raised the peak to 450 feet in two weeks, to 930 feet in eight months and to 1,020 feet in two years. By 1952, when it stopped erupting, it was 1,350 feet high and the nearby villages of Parícutin and Parangaricutiro had been smothered under debris from the new mountain. Lava flows spread as much as six miles from the crater" (Lorus J. Milne, *Life Nature Library: The Mountains,* New York: Time, Inc., 1962, p. 37; see also James A. Green, "Parícutin, the Cornfield That Grew a Volcano," *National Geographic Magazine,* Feb., 1944, pp. 129-64).

Sidney P. Clementson, a British engineer, has analyzed the published studies of rock samples from twelve volcanoes in Russia and ten samples from other places around the world which show ages from 100 million to 10 billion years by typical radioactive dating methods, whereas it is known that these volcanic rocks were formed within the past 200 years! Clementson concludes that "calculated ages give no indication whatever of the age of the host rocks. In cases where calculated ages are millions of years, the rocks could be quite young. Furthermore, these ages have no relationship to the age of the earth, because of course, the various ages computed have varied so widely. Consequently ratios of parent and daughter elements are merely ratios, and their use as a base for projecting 'ages' of the rocks, or of the earth itself, is highly questionable and fraught with many assumptions that cannot be checked. This conclusion would fit the concept of a young earth and a recent creation as deduced from the Bible" ("A Critical Examination of Radioactive Dating of Rocks," *Creation Research Society Quarterly,* Dec., 1970, p. 141).

What applies to evolution applies also to uniformitarianism,[46] for both concepts are purely naturalistic extrapolations into the realm of cosmogony in defiance of the Biblical doctrines of supernatural creation and catastrophism. It is our firm conviction that these doctrines have not been disproved by science, but have simply been rejected and ignored. The apostle Peter prophesied this very thing when he said that those who would "in the last days" deny the Flood in favor of uniformitarianism would do so not because of impelling scientific evidences, but rather because they *wish* (Greek— *thelontas*) it to be so (II Peter 3:5)! The impact of this statement may be better appreciated by this spectrum of translations:

> "willingly are ignorant of" (AV)
> "wilfully forget" (ASV)
> "deliberately ignore" (RSV)
> "wilfully shut their eyes to the fact that" (TCNT)
> "deliberately shutting their eyes to a fact that they
>   know very well" (Phillips)
> "they are fain to forget" (Knox)

As Christians who believe that the Word of God speaks to us with final authority, not only in the realm of the spiritual, but also in the realm of the historical and the scientific, it is our infinite privilege, by the grace of God in Christ, to test all things by this infallible revelation of truth. Only then may we expect to be delivered from the terrible bondage of error into the realm of light that is the exclusive domain of the God of creation and revelation.

---

46. While not at all endorsing the motives and mechanisms of Immanuel Velikovsky's concepts of global catastrophism (though many valuable insights may be gained especially from his *Earth in Upheaval*), we find it fascinating to observe the response of the uniformitarian establishment to his writings. If even a secular alternative to uniformitarianism is so fanatically suppressed, one can well imagine how *Biblical* catastrophism would fare in such circles! See Alfred de Grazia, *The Velikovsky Affair* (New Hyde Park, N.Y.: University Books, 1966), and the special May 1972 and Fall 1972 issues of *Pensee* (P.O. Box 414, Portland, Ore. 97207). See also Norman Macbeth, *Darwin Retried,* pp. 110-16.

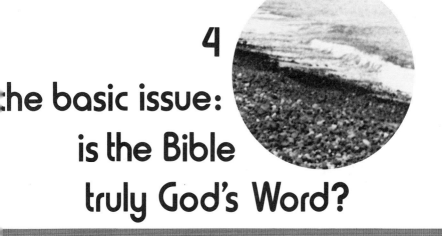

4

the basic issue:
is the Bible
truly God's Word?

IF THE COMPLEXITY of living things and of all energy systems in the universe logically *excludes* cosmic evolutionism (especially in the light of the second law of thermodynamics), then the world-wide evidence of mass extinctions of animals, vast sedimentary strata, enormous lava flows, frozen tundras and arctic zones, and recently uplifted mountain ranges *excludes* the uniformist concept of earth history as popularly held by geologists today.

But many of us are painfully aware of the mysterious incapacity of the human mind to draw correct metaphysical and theological conclusions from empirical observation. He is self-deceived who believes that his ultimate world-and-life view is reached through a careful and unbiased sifting of all the relevant data of sense experience and logic! History has demonstrated clearly that *all* leading men of science have been *completely* in error in interpreting various important facets of our universe. And, even more disastrously, *all* leading theologians during certain eras of church history have been in *complete* error in their interpretation of important doctrines of the Christian faith as set forth in Scripture. The possibilities for error in the two realms of science and theology are simply enormous, for correct interpretations of natural phenomena and Biblical passages are usually balanced delicately upon a complex substructure of previously validated assumptions and methodologies. In a word: correct conclusions in the modern Bible/science controversy depend upon correct starting points.

For a Christian, the written Word of God, correctly interpreted, must be the starting point for arriving at valid conclusions in every significant realm of meaning. If the God-honored and time-honored method of grammatical-historical ("normal") interpretation of the Bible is valid, then Biblical statements of history and doctrine cannot be twisted at the whim of the interpreter. Even during the apostolic era this practice was all too prevalent, and was denounced by the apostle Peter in powerful terms: "our beloved brother Paul . . . wrote unto you . . . in all his epistles . . . wherein are some things hard to be understood, which the ignorant and unstedfast wrest, as they do also the other scriptures, unto their own destruction" (II Peter 3:15-16). It should be especially noted that Peter considered such twisting and ignoring of Scripture as leading "unto their own destruction." Thus, the interpretation of God's Word is not a playful pastime but frighteningly serious business for Christians.

the basic issue: is the Bible truly God's Word? • 95

This is especially true of Genesis, the foundational book of the Bible, including its oft-twisted first eleven chapters. With a few exceptions,[1] all New Testament books refer to Genesis 1-11. Also, *every chapter* of Genesis 1-11 is referred to somewhere in the New Testament. Furthermore, *every New Testament writer* refers to Genesis 1-11. And finally, *the Lord Jesus Christ referred to each of the first seven chapters of Genesis.*[2]

The careful student of God's Word knows full well that he must stand before the Judgment Seat of Christ to be judged for the way he has handled Scripture (Rom. 14:10, 12; I Cor. 3:10-15; II Cor. 5:10; Rev. 22:18-19). A Christian may be excused for his ignorance of the details of astrophysics, geology, microbiology, or genetics—for in this age of specialization, no one can know everything about his own field, to say nothing of all other significant branches of science![3] But he will *not* be excused for his willful ignorance of God's revealed Word:

> And he answered and said, Have ye not read . . . ? (Matt. 19:4).
>
> And Jesus saith unto them, Yea: did ye never read . . . ? (Matt. 21:16).
>
> Ye do err, not knowing the scriptures, nor the power of God (Matt. 22:29).
>
> Have ye not read even this scripture . . . ? (Mark 12:15).
>
> If they hear not Moses and the prophets, neither will they be persuaded, if one rise from the dead (Luke 16:31).
>
> And he said unto them, O foolish men, and slow of heart to believe in all that the prophets have spoken! (Luke 24:25).
>
> If ye believed Moses, ye would believe me; for he wrote of me. But if ye believe not his writings, how shall ye believe my words? (John 5:46-47).
>
> He that . . . receiveth not my sayings, hath one that judgeth him: the word that I spake, the same shall judge him in the last day (John 12:48).
>
> Not walking in craftiness, nor handling the word of God deceitfully (II Cor. 4:2).
>
> Give diligence to present thyself approved unto God, a work-

---

1. Philippians, Thessalonians, II Timothy, Titus, Philemon, II and III John.
2. Henry M. Morris, *The Remarkable Birth of the Planet Earth* (San Diego: Institute for Creation Research, 1972), p. 103.
3. It has been estimated that 50,000 significant articles in the field of mathematics alone are published each year!

man that needeth not to be ashamed, handling aright the word of truth (II Tim. 2:15).

In the last days mockers shall come with mockery, walking after their own lusts, and saying, ... all things continue as they were from the beginning of the creation. For this they wilfully forget ... wherein are some things hard to be understood, which the ignorant and unstedfast wrest, as they do also the other scriptures, unto their own destruction. (II Peter 3:3-5, 16).

Mature Christians, who are adequately taught in God's Word, have no fear of historical, archaeological, or scientific discoveries which appear to nullify any portion or any statement of infallible Scripture. "For verily I say unto you, Till heaven and earth pass away, one jot or one tittle shall in no wise pass away from the law, till all things be accomplished" (Matt. 5:18). One hundred years of archaeological research in the Bible lands—and this represents only a scratching of the surface of potential discovery[4]—has more than vindicated those who have placed their confidence in the historical and geographical statements of Scripture. True faith in the Word of God does not *depend* upon such confirmations, but they do provide a certain sense of intellectual satisfaction and they do help to provide background illumination for various places, persons, and events in the Bible.

A special case in point is the general theory of evolution. By the turn of the century there was hardly a scientist of note who dared to raise a voice against Darwin's concept that all living things (including man) had evolved by natural (or "providential") processes from a tiny, simple, marine organism. Zoologists and biologists had spoken. The vast majority of educated men bowed in homage. Enormous pressure was thus applied to the intelligent Christian to conform and to compromise the Genesis creation account to this nearly unanimous opinion of leading scientists.

But many Christians were not willing to bow to such pressures, because of their deep conviction that some day, in God's good time, new light would be shed on the areas of apparent conflict between Scripture and the natural sciences. And that faith and confidence has been remarkably vindicated. Large cracks have already become visible in the fortress of "amoeba to man" evolutionism, so that even

---

4. See Edwin Yamauchi, *The Stones and the Scriptures* (Philadelphia: J. B. Lippincott Co., 1972), pp. 146-57.

secular writers such as G. A. Kerkut[5] and Norman Macbeth[6] are raising serious and eloquent objections to the entire Neo-Darwinian structure. And Christian students now have at hand dozens of outstanding works written by competent Christian men of science that reveal the fallacies of not only the *general* theory of evolution (macro-evolution) but also of certain aspects of the *special* theory of evolution (micro-evolution) as well. Compromise positions, such as theistic evolution, have been recognized by increasing numbers of Christians to be dangerous and quite unnecessary concessions to the enemies of God's Word.[7]

But if the Genesis concept of "created kinds" has been greatly clarified and vindicated through scientific discoveries and theological debates since 1950,[8] then what can be said for the equally important concepts of a recently created earth and a universal Flood in the days of Noah? The *manner* in which God brought living things into existence (i.e., by direct creation rather than by evolutionary processes) is quite clearly stated in Genesis. But the *order* in which these things happened (e.g., fruit trees before marine creatures) and the amount of *time* involved in these events (six literal days; cf. Exod. 20:11) are also clearly stated in Genesis. And it is precisely the order and duration of these creation events that call for an earth of comparatively recent origin and a catastrophe of global scale (or, to be more exact, a year-long complex of millions of catastrophes) at the dawn of human history.

Christians who are committed to the historical/grammatical system of Biblical interpretation (and what other system can be seriously considered?) cannot shelve the question of the length of the creation days and the question of the magnitude of the Flood, any more than they can ignore the question of whether or not Christ was born in Bethlehem (once it is agreed that he was born of a virgin). The Christian interpreter, following the example of Christ and the apostles, is committed to the *entirety* of Bible history, not just to certain points here and there. Similarly, no scientist worthy of the name could seriously promote a theory that deliberately ignored clear evidences to the contrary. An interpretive

---

5. G. A. Kerkut, *Implications of Evolution* (New York: Pergamon Press, 1960).
6. Norman Macbeth, *Darwin Retried* (Boston: Gambit, Inc., 1972).
7. Cf. Henry M. Morris, "Theistic Evolution," *Creation Research Society Quarterly,* March, 1972, pp. 269-72.
8. Cf. J. C. Whitcomb, Jr., *The Early Earth* (Grand Rapids: Baker Book House, 1972), pp. 77-91.

scheme that refuses to incorporate *all* the facts must be abandoned.

Especially since the early 1960s, the Christian public has been alerted to the necessity of a *Biblically consistent and therefore ultimate challenge to naturalistic scientism,* through the writings of such scientists as Henry M. Morris, Duane T. Gish, George F. Howe, Walter E. Lammerts, John N. Moore, John W. Klotz, William J. Tinkle, Thomas G. Barnes, Paul A. Zimmerman, Harold S. Slusher, George W. Mulfinger, Wilbert H. Rusch, Sr., Frank L. Marsh, Melvin A. Cook, Bolton Davidheiser, and Robert V. Gentry, to name but a few. For even though the mechanisms of evolution may be challenged, and though embarrassing gaps in the fossil record may be exposed to view, faith and hope in the Neo-Darwinian system somehow continues to flourish in the hearts of its adherents. But when the *time-scale of evolutionary history* is also challenged, and the billions of years of earth history are suddenly *reduced to mere thousands of years,* Neo-Darwinians are reduced to despair. Charles Darwin himself understood this clearly; for when Lord Kelvin (William Thomson) insisted that the earth could be no more than fifteen or twenty million years old,

> ...he referred to Lord Kelvin as an "odious specter" and feared that Darwinism was finished if Kelvin was correct: "I am greatly troubled at the short duration of the world according to Lord Kelvin, for I require for my theoretical views a very long period."[9]

Thus, when John W. Klotz exposed the shallowness of typical evolutionary arguments in his monumental *Genes, Genesis and Evolution,* his work might have been much more widely received (even in Christian circles mildly committed to theistic evolutionism) except for such electrifying statements as this: "Scripture indicates that the age of the earth must be measured in thousands rather than millions and billions of years."[10]

Biblical Catastrophism versus Uniformitarianism

It is, of course, the historical geologists (i.e., geologists who specialize in earth history) who have fought the greatest

9. Norman Macbeth, *Darwin Retried* (Boston: Gambit, Inc., 1971), p. 109.
10. John W. Klotz, *Genes, Genesis, and Evolution* (St. Louis: Concordia Pub. House, 1955), pp. 114, 116. In the 1970 revised edition, this statement is found on page 113.

UNIFORMITARIANISM AND A BURNING CANDLE

Many scientists claim to have nearly infallible methods for determining the age of the earth and its various formations. But all of these methods are built upon two basic and unprovable assumptions: (1) the assumption of starting point or original condition and (2) the assumption of a uniform rate of change from that starting point to the present.

Consider a burning candle in an abandoned house. It is now burning at the rate of one inch an hour. *Question:* How long has it been burning and, thus, how long ago was the house abandoned? *Answer:* No one can know until it can be shown how high the candle was when it was last lit and how fast it was burning originally!

Question: How old is the earth? *Answer:* No one can know unless it can be shown what it was like when it began and how rapidly it has changed since then! If it began as a molten mass of rock and metal and has been cooling down at a steady rate, it would be millions of years old. *But if we accept God's record in Genesis, it was created with a cool crust and liquid oceans.* Thus, it would not have required millions of years for the crust and oceans to form. This is perfectly reasonable, because the earth was created to be a home for man (Ps. 115:16, Isa. 45:18). Did God have to wait millions (or billions) of years to accomplish this? If God could create Adam and Eve "full-grown," did He have less power to create a "full-grown" earth? Since uniformitarians do not really know where even an original molten mass of rock and metal could have come from, there is no truly rational alternative to the creationist model. For a fascinating analysis of the entire problem by a scientist/theologian, see Charles A. Clough, *Laying the Foundation* (Lubbock, Texas: Lubbock Bible Church [3202 34th St.], 1973), pp. 1-133.

battles against the concept of a global Deluge at the beginning of human history. It is not that their uniformitarian philosophy forces them to deny any and all catastrophes, for uniformitarianism today is much more flexible than it used to be. In the words of one geologist:

> In the early days of geology uniformity not only implied the idea of the continuity of natural laws through time (methodological uniformitarianism) but also the idea that the processes of the past were only of the same kind and the same rate as processes of the present (substantive uniformitarianism). The latter idea developed as an extreme reaction to the widespread catastrophism of the 18th and 19th centuries. It has no basis in fact and is rejected by virtually all geologists today.[11]

When Christian (and other) geologists are accused of being "uniformitarians," they frequently register a strong protest lest their position be confused with the extreme positions held by some uniformitarian geologists of earlier days.[12]

The sensitivity of many historical geologists to criticisms from those outside their professional circle may be illustrated in the following manner. In *The Genesis Flood,* the authors carefully defined their use of the term "uniformitarianism," seeking to make it perfectly clear that while many modern proponents of this concept *do* allow for various widespread catastrophes throughout earth history, such as enormous lava flows (which must be explained, at all costs, in purely naturalistic terms), they do *not* allow for such supernatural, global catastrophes as the great Flood described in Genesis

---

11. Davis A. Young, review of *Symposium on Creation—II,* by Donald W. Patten, in *Westminster Theological Journal,* Nov., 1971, p. 65. See also Clifford L. Burdick, "The Structure and Fabric of Geology," *Creation Research Society Quarterly,* Dec., 1970, p. 143, with special reference to his quotation from Norman Newell's 1963 address to the American Geological Institute (reported also in *Newsweek,* Dec. 23, 1963, p. 48).

12. Similarly, evolutionary anthropologists often resist the claim that they are deriving men from apes. Their answer is that men did *not* come from apes, but rather both men *and* apes have descended from a common sub-human ancestral population! "This is supposed to make an important difference. But the fact is that evolutionists in general and Charles Darwin in particular have made it a matter of record in print that they *do* believe we evolved from monkeys or apes or both." Dr. Bolton Davidheiser proceeds to give several citations from such protesters and also from those who openly admit to this position. *Evolution and Christian Faith* (Nutley, N.J.: Presbyterian & Reformed Pub. Co., 1969), pp. 24 ff.

or the final destruction of the world described in II Peter 3 and other passages. In fact, they really *cannot* allow for any miraculous interventions by God into the natural fabric of cause and effect relationships in this supposedly "closed universe" and still be classified as uniformitarians.[13]

Christians who understand Scripture are well aware of the fact that the Bible points to the validity of uniformitarianism in a limited sense during the post-Deluge and pre-eschatological era in which we *now* live (e.g., II Peter 3:7—"the heavens that now are, and the earth, by the same word have been stored up for fire, being reserved against the day of judgment . . ."). This especially applies to present-day *geological* processes (e.g., the rate of the earth's rotation and its tilt of axis—Gen. 8:22), *astronomical* processes (e.g., the movements of celestial bodies—Jer. 33:20, 25),[14] and *meteorological* processes (cf. Eccles. 1:6 and Matt. 16:2, 3).

Furthermore, within the framework of this God-guaranteed phase of earth history—this "limited uniformitarianism phase" —full allowance is made in Scripture for various types of non-miraculous local catastrophes, such as earthquakes (e.g., Amos 1:1, Zech. 14:5), floods, volcanic eruptions, enormous meteorite impacts, etc. Special effort was made by the authors of *The Genesis Flood* to clarify this point.[15]

In addition, Biblical catastrophism maintains that uniformitarian processes must be the *normal* and *characteristic* pattern of God's providential control of the earth *throughout* its history, or else miracles would lose their identity and sign-value by virtue of the very frequency and familiarity of their occurrence. "Miraculous intervention acquires significance only against the backdrop of a basic pattern of uniformity."[16]

Finally, the authors of *The Genesis Flood* emphasized that

---

13. On this basis, it is difficult to understand how any consistent Christian can be even a "methodological uniformitarian" in the ultimate sense of that term. On the other hand, Immanuel Velikovsky (and to some extent, Donald Patten) can advocate *a global catastrophe* several thousand years ago and still be classified as a "methodological uniformitarian," because he denies divine miracles and the historicity of the Book of Genesis. It must be emphasized that Biblical catastrophism is just as much concerned with the *cause* of the Flood as with its *magnitude*.

14. Cf. J. C. Whitcomb, Jr., *Solomon to the Exile* (Grand Rapids: Baker Book House, 1971), pp. 127-29, for evidence that the return of the shadow on King Hezekiah's sundial was a localized miracle of light refraction, and that the "long day" of Joshua 10:12-14 must be explained in similar fashion.

15. See pages 124, 131, 137, 287, 312, 313, 328.

16. Whitcomb and Morris, *The Genesis Flood,* p. xxi, note No. 1.

Biblical catastrophism, to the extent that it contradicts geologic uniformitarianism, applies only to those *rare* historical
cases where God *"on the occasions mentioned in Scripture"*
(especially during the Creation Week and the year of the
Flood) "directly intervened in the normal physical processes
of the universe, causing significant changes therein *for a
time.*"[17] And yet, Dr. Davis A. Young, a Christian geologist
who rejects the global Flood view, says practically the same
thing:

> The fact that God does intervene occasionally does not in-
> validate methodological uniformitarianism as a basic guid-
> ing principle for understanding those stretches of time when
> God did not intervene! The extrapolation of present laws
> into the past is a legitimate method for the Christian geolo-
> gist, in the reviewer's opinion, except in those cases where
> Scripture unequivocally indicates a direct act of God. There
> is nothing in Scripture which rules out this basically, albeit
> punctuated, uniformitarian approach.[18]

Is this not an inconsistency? Would any prominent "methodological uniformitarian geologist" allow his system of earth
history, even for a moment, to be "punctuated" by "a direct
act of God"? But even more important, by what exegetical or
hermeneutical principle does Dr. Young determine that the
Flood was neither global nor "a direct act of God"? We do
not have to seek far for the answer. He apparently does not
need to scrutinize the text of Scripture at all. And why not?
Because geologists have spoken! "Geologists today, however,
have rejected the global flood catastrophe as a compre-
hensive principle of explanation, not so much because of any
philosophical prejudice, but simply because the evidence has
not been found."[19]

Though we have shown that there *is* a great deal of evidence for a global Flood, that is not the main issue at this
point. Our first answer to Dr. Young is God's word through
the apostle Peter, that those who would deny the fact that
the world was once destroyed by a flood would do so because
they *wish* to do so. Thus, denial of the Flood in our day *is*
because of philosophical prejudice, from God's viewpoint.

17. Whitcomb and Morris, *Flood,* p. xxi.
18. Davis A. Young, review of *Symposium on Creation—II,* Donald
    W. Patten, ed., in *Westminster Theological Journal,* Vol. 34, No.
    1 (Nov., 1971), p. 65.
19. Young, p. 65. For an almost identical statement, see Roger J.
    Cuffey, "Reaction and Rebuttal," *JASA,* March, 1971, p. 24.

Second, we might remind Dr. Young that the evidence for man's direct creation from the dust hasn't been found either, and yet he is willing to write: "The Christian must battle to the death the notion that man has evolved from nonhuman animal life."[20] Is it our privilege as Christians to decide *which* direct acts of God we will defend "to the death"? Must Christians give up the Biblical doctrine of a universal Flood simply because certain geologists insist that "the evidence has not been found"?

Thus, Biblical catastrophism does *not* undermine all the historical sciences; it does *not* introduce irrational and unpredictable factors into the otherwise normal processes of the universe; and it does *not* ignore the flexibility of modern-style historical geologists in their willingness to allow some major (but not supernatural!) catastrophes in the past. In the light of this positional statement by the authors of *The Genesis Flood,* what must be said about comments like the following, written by recognized evangelical scholars in published reviews?

> The authors flog "uniformitarianism" from beginning to end. ... But, taken to its logical conclusion, the authors' approach would completely destroy the scientific method. If I wanted to be shockingly blunt, I might ask Dr. Morris, "Why do you bother studying and teaching engineering?" All scientific law is based on uniformitarianism. It is only the dogmatism of science that we must oppose. Even the authors do not hesitate to draw on science hundreds of times to support their arguments![21]

The following words were written by "a theologically trained Christian educator outside the camp of professional geologists."

> In several specific areas the arguments of the book fall short. First of all, a false definition of uniformitarianism is set up as a "straw-man." ... The fact of the matter is that geologists hold that the laws of physics and chemistry remain unchanged with time, but that the rates of geomorphic processes have varied and do vary widely. This is particularly well recognized today in tectonics and paleontology.[22]

---

20. Davis A. Young, review of *Evolution and Christian Faith* by Bolton Davidheiser, in *The Westminster Theological Journal,* Vol. 23, No. 2 (May, 1971), p. 223.
21. William Sanford LaSor, review of *The Genesis Flood,* in *Eternity,* August, 1961, p. 43.
22. Frank H. Roberts, review of *The Genesis Flood* in the *Journal of the American Scientific Affiliation,* March, 1964, p. 28.

These statements, by Christian scholars, are all too typical of the fundamental and widespread misunderstanding of the enormous chasm that separates true Biblical catastrophism on the one hand from uniformitarianism (of whatever form—substantive or methodological) on the other hand. These concepts are not simply different in degree. *They are different in kind.* One honors the total testimony of inspired Scripture. The other manipulates Scripture in the light of human logic and experience, or else ignores it completely.

Are Geologists Superior to Scripture?

One of the most serious problems in the current debate on the Genesis Flood is the unshakable confidence which many Christian men of science seem to have in the uniformitarian concept of earth history. Such men seem to be saying that the currently popular geologic timetable must be maintained at all costs if Christianity is to be made credible to the twentieth-century mind!

Thus, after insisting that he believes in the verbal inspiration of the Bible and the reality of miracles, one Christian geologist boldly asserts: "But to me as a professional geologist the Bible does not teach catastrophism."[23] But what special skill in the science of Bible interpretation does one acquire by virtue of being a "professional geologist"? Does a study of historical geology in the average university automatically equip one to handle the Hebrew and Greek text of sacred Scripture? Must the Christian set aside all the God-honored and time-honored laws of Biblical hermeneutics and exegesis which he has learned through years of patient study of the original text whenever a *geologist* enters the scene and begins to make authoritative pronouncements on what the Book of Genesis can or cannot be saying to us? Certainly a geologist has a right to believe or reject what he chooses, but that is not the question at issue. Our assertion is that even though he may reject the concept of a global Flood if he so chooses, he does not have the right to be accepted as an authoritative voice when he says that "the Bible does not teach catastrophism."

The same geologist goes on to say: "It is very significant that Christian geologists have not praised *The Genesis Flood* as have other Christians."[24] But what does this imply? That only Christian geologists possess the key of knowledge by

---

23. Wayne U. Ault, review of *The Genesis Flood,* in the *Journal of the American Scientific Affiliation,* March, 1964, p. 29.
24. Ault, p. 29.

which Biblical truth must be judged? Should every large church and every Christian institution of higher learning have a geologist on its staff in order to expedite the all-important task of expounding those many portions of Scripture that deal with origins and pre-Abrahamic history? In addition to the illuminating work of the Holy Spirit (I John 2:27), persistent prayer (Ps. 119:18), and interpretive skill that comes through a patient comparison of Scripture with Scripture (Acts 17:11, I Cor. 2:12-16, II Tim. 2:15), must all true Bible students add one additional qualification, namely, official approval from professional geologists for all interpretations that touch on pre-Abrahamic history?

Few Christian geologists seem to have thought through the full implications of such a development. We would, first of all, need to provide for all Christians a new "amplified version" of some of the most familiar statements of our Lord, so that they might read as follows:

> Ye do err, not knowing the Scriptures, nor the power of God, *nor the general consensus of mid-twentieth century geological opinion concerning earth history* (Matt. 22:29 "amplified").

> O fools and slow of heart to believe all that the prophets *and twentieth century geologists* have spoken (Luke 24:25 "amplified.")

We are *not* suggesting that any Christian geologist would tolerate for a moment such a tampering with the text of Scripture. Nor are we questioning the stupendous contribution that *the science of geology* has made, under God's providence, to our understanding of the earth's features and its natural processes during *this phase* of its existence (since the Flood and until the Second Coming of Christ).[25] What we *are*

---

25. "We do not presume to· question any of the data of geological *science*. Science (meaning 'knowledge') necessarily can deal only with *present* processes, which can be measured and evaluated at the present time; the 'scientific method' by definition involves experimental reproducibility. Thus, extrapolation of present processes into the prehistoric past or into the eschatological future is not really science.... In the second place, we emphatically do not question uniformity of the basic laws of physics.... These laws are basic in geology and in all science, and are clearly set forth in Scripture. This is the *true* principle of uniformity. We only question the assumption of uniformity of *rates* of geological and other processes, and even here essentially only as required by Biblical revelation." Whitcomb and Morris, in "Preface to the Sixth Printing" of *The Genesis Flood* (1964), pp. xxvi, xxvii.

PETRIFIED LOGS

"There lie thousands of fossilized logs, many of them broken up into short segments, others complete and unbroken. . . . The average diameter of the logs is 3 to 4 feet, and the length 60 to 80 feet. Some logs 7 feet in greatest diameter and 125 feet long have been observed. None are standing in position of growth but, with branches stripped, *lie scattered about as though floated by running water until stranded and subsequently buried in the places where they are now found.* The original forests may have been scores of miles distant. The cell structure and fibers have been almost perfectly preserved by molecular replacement of silica . . . ." (Raymond C. Moore, *Introduction to Historical Geology,* 2nd ed.; New York: McGraw-Hill, 1958, pp. 401-02. Italics added.)

Petrified logs have been an enigma to many scientists. The evidences point rather clearly to catastrophic conditions that prevailed at the time of the Flood, when these thousands of trunks were transported and grounded in huge log jams. Many of the trunks appear to have the bark intact, indicating rapid burial before rotting could occur. The wood tissue is very well preserved as agate. Foliage has been stripped from the trunks. *This was no local catastrophe,* because these types of fossil trees from the "Triassic" are widespread over the Southwest. No geologist insists that the "forest" is *in situ,* and it is obvious that petrified logs are not being formed anywhere in the world today. (The author hereby expresses appreciation to Mr. Stuart Nevins, a graduate student in geology, for his assistance in analyzing the significance of petrified logs.)

suggesting is that many Christian geologists have failed to make that all-important distinction between geology as a *science* and geology as a pseudo-scientific *philosophy.*

To make such a distinction we need, of course, help from beyond ourselves and our fellow-scientists. In fact, we need *divinely provided infallible guidelines* to enable us to avoid futile and irrelevant enterprises and concepts that empiricism, in the very nature of the case, cannot discern.[26] And true Christians are persuaded that *they have these guidelines in Holy Scripture!* Furthermore, Protestants have traditionally contended that Scripture is not only divinely *authoritative* but also *perspicuous* in its statements.[27] Otherwise, Christians would be subjected to the tyranny of various self-appointed "experts," apart from whose approval we could not really take God at His Word. Surely no geologist who is a consistent Christian would desire to see God's Word reduced to utter irrelevance. But if the Bible is not allowed *to interpret itself,* that is exactly what must happen.

For two or three generations following Darwin, it was the "Christian biologists" that persuaded the church and its theologians to accommodate Genesis to the general theory of

---

26. Davis A. Young has rightly criticised Richard H. Bube (*The Encounter Between Christianity and Science,* Grand Rapids: Wm. B. Eerdmans Pub. Co., 1968) for his low view of Scripture. Young states: "If Scripture is unequivocal in teaching one 'hypothesis' concerning a certain fact then all other hypotheses are *irrelevant.* For example the hypothesis that Jesus had a human father is irrelevant. Similarly (at the risk of offending some of our evangelical friends) we may state that the evolution of man from lower animals is an irrelevant hypothesis. In short the Christian geologist must insist on invoking the special creation hypothesis where Scripture insists on it." (*Westminster Theological Journal,* May, 1969, p. 223). Exactly so! And this is precisely why we insist that since Scripture clearly teaches the concept of a global Flood at the dawn of human history, *any hypothesis of historical geology that ignores the hydrodynamic significance of a year-long global Flood is irrelevant!* It is disappointing that Dr. Young does not recognize the inconsistency of his local Flood position at this point. See Davis A. Young, "Some Practical Geological Problems in the Application of the Mature Creation Doctrine," *W.T.J.* (May, 1973, pp. 268-80) and this writer's reply in the Fall, 1973 issue of the same journal.
27. "An obscure book could not perform the functions Scripture would perform. A denial of perspicuity is a denial of the *sola scriptura* principle itself.... Whenever a church or theologian [or a geologist!—J.C.W.] takes it upon himself to define truth without reference to the objective authority of God's Word, he becomes demonically solipsistic." Clark H. Pinnock, *Biblical Revelation* (Chicago: Moody Press, 1971), p. 99.

evolution. But it is quite obvious that this was a premature surrender, even from a scientific standpoint, for we now have the writings of a number of highly qualified geneticists and biologists who totally reject the Neo-Darwinian concept.[28] As the horizons of genetics, bio-chemistry, and paleontology have expanded, it has become more and more obvious that those theologians who molded God's infallible Word to fit "the general consensus of biological opinion" concerning origins blundered tragically and led the Church into a lower view of the authority of God's Word. Only eternity will reveal the full extent of this theological disaster. Should not this serve as a clear warning to all true Christians that theoretical geology is no more sacrosanct in the 1970's than was theoretical biology in the 1940's or theoretical astronomy in the 1920's?

A Dutch Geologist Versus The Genesis Flood

All Christians may be thankful for the significant background light that the science of Biblical archaeology has been able to shed on previously obscure passages of Scripture. But what kind of "light" are certain Christian geologists attempting to shed upon the statements of God's Word?

J. R. van de Fliert, who has been Professor of Historical and Tectonical Geology at the Free University of Amsterdam since 1960, has gained a wide reputation for his rejection of Biblical catastrophism in favor of uniformitarianism. When asked to write a definitive refutation of Whitcomb and Morris, *The Genesis Flood,* he "felt very reluctant to write against it, but finally agreed to do so, yielding to stress from different sides." The result was a rather lengthy article entitled, "Fundamentalism and the Fundamentals of Geology," which has been considered by some scientists and theologians to be the ultimate word on the subject of "Flood geology."[29]

---

28. See, for example, A. E. Wilder Smith, *The Creation of Life* (Wheaton, Ill.: Harold Shaw Pub., 1970); and Duane T. Gish, *Speculations and Experiments Related to Theories on the Origin of Life* (San Diego, Calif.: Institute for Creation Research, 2716 Madison Ave., San Diego 92116; 1972). See also the references listed on p. 64, Note 35.

29. Thus, A. N. Triton (Review of *The Genesis Flood* in *The Christian Graduate,* Vol. 22, No. 4, 1969, p. 28) challenges his readers to "see the devastating review by the highly orthodox reformed Christian Professor van de Fliert in the *International Reformed Bulletin.*" Dr. Clarence Menninga of Calvin College ("His Word and His World," *The Banner,* Nov. 27, 1970, p. 15) is confident that "the arguments from the fossil record which (Morris and Whitcomb) present have been refuted by J. R. van de Fliert." See

Appearing first in the Spring, 1968, issue of *The International Reformed Bulletin,* it was reprinted in the September, 1969, issue of *The Journal of the American Scientific Affiliation* and the Autumn, 1970, issue of *Faith and Thought* (Journal of the Victoria Institute).

Probably speaking for the majority of Christian geologists in the American Scientific Affiliation, Dr. Roger J. Cuffey of the Department of Geology and Geophysics at the Pennsylvania State University, commented:

> First, the over-all impression one gets from reading this article is that (finally!) here is a widely experienced professional geologist, who—even though an evangelical Christian—accepts the findings of modern geology, and who carefully explains why the pseudo-scientific flood-geologists are wrong (in terms which most informed laymen will understand). I believe that it is very important to put the views of such men as van de Fliert before the Christian public, so that they are not so likely to be misled by the erroneous views of people (like the flood geologists) ignorant of modern earth science.[30]

Dr. Cuffey concludes that Professor van de Fliert's article "adequately rebuts the anti-uniformitarianism so widely accepted among evangelical scholars; *consequently, I see no need to further comment on this erroneous view of earth science.*"[31]

Dr. William F. Tanner, a Christian "consulting geologist," agreed that the article was excellent, but "the case could be made much stronger than van de Fliert makes it." In fact, his position "is quite moderate, rather than extreme."[32]

Dr. Donald C. Boardman, head of the geology department at Wheaton College, exclaimed:

> It is time for scientists who are Christians to speak up and be counted in regard to "flood geology" and interpretations of the Scriptures. Van de Fliert is absolutely right when he

---

also James Moore, "Charles Lyell and the Noachian Deluge," *JASA,* Sept., 1970, p. 114; and Richard Bube, *The Human Quest* (Waco, Texas: Word, Inc., 1971), p. 189.

30. Roger J. Cuffey, comment on "Fundamentalism and the Fundamentals of Geology," by J. R. van de Fliert, *JASA,* Sept., 1969, p. 71.
31. Roger J. Cuffey, "Critique of 'The Dying of the Giants,'" by William A. Springstead, *JASA,* Sept., 1970, p. 96. Italics added.
32. William F. Tanner, comment on "Fundamentalism and the Fundamentals of Geology," by J. R. van de Fliert, *JASA,* Sept., 1969, p. 73.

says that "We deal a death blow to the Christian religion when we bring the Holy Scriptures down to scientific level by teaching that the Bible should give us a kind of scientific world picture or axiomata of historical geology. . . ."[33]

With such recommendations many Christian people have undoubtedly turned to Professor van de Fliert's article with anticipations of finding *final answers* on the vital questions that have confronted Christians in the great Genesis/geology conflict of modern times. In harmonizing the Biblical account with historical geology, one would naturally expect some new Biblical evidence that the days of Genesis were actually ages or that there really was a gap of enormous time between the first two verses or between some other verses in Genesis chapter one as well as some perspicuous exegesis demonstrating conclusively that the Biblical account describes a local rather than a global Flood. But are such solutions (or even attempted solutions) found in the article? No! Professor van de Fliert "resolves" the conflict once and for all by informing us that there never has been a conflict at all! Genesis 1-11 can be interpreted any way we choose because its statements can neither be proven nor disproven by science! It is a purely religious document, even as Karl Barth, Emil Brunner, Rudolph Bultmann, and other Neo-orthodox and existentialist theologians have been insisting for years! So now, at long last, in the "light" of this great discovery, "Christian astronomers, geologists, and biologists can work *without fear* as long as they respect the limits of their own scientific field."[34]

Thus, to use Cuffey's description of van de Fliert, "a widely experienced professional geologist, who—even though an evangelical Christian—accepts the finding of modern geology," *effectively evaporates the early chapters of Genesis without the use of a single exegetical, contextual, or theological argument!* The article of van de Fliert begins with this amazing pronouncement:

> Any attempt to harmonize the historical geology of today with the account of the first chapters of Genesis represents a misunderstanding of the Genesis record. . . . The Bible does not give outlines of historical geology nor accounts of scientifically controllable creative acts of God! . . . Christians who do believe in God . . . corrupt scientific work thoroughly when they start from pretended biblical (in fact, imposed by

33. Tanner, p. 75.
34. J. R. van de Fliert, "Fundamentalism and the Fundamentals of Geology," *JASA,* Sept., 1969, p. 80.

the basic issue: is the Bible truly God's Word? • 113

STALACTITES AND STALAGMITES
UNDER THE LINCOLN MEMORIAL

A "curtain" of stalactites grows from the foundation ceiling beneath the Lincoln Memorial in Washington, D.C. (left photo). Some of the stalactites, formed from deposition of calcium carbonate ($CaCO_3$), range to about *five feet in length*. The Lincoln Memorial was built in 1923 and this photograph was taken on February 12, 1968.

A stalagmite and its companion stalactite (right photo) grow toward each other beneath the Lincoln Memorial. In time, they will join to form a mineral link between ceiling and floor.

The growth rate of dripstone formations in many caves today is much slower than this, but even in caves a very slow rate of growth cannot be assumed to be either typical or uniform. The enormous ages generally assigned to such formations in caves ignores the extreme variability of such factors as (1) rate of water drip; (2) concentration of salts in solution; (3) the types of salts in solution, i.e., their solubility; (4) the rate of evaporation of water; (5) the rate of evaporation of carbon dioxide; and (6) the degree of evaporation (partial or complete). Thus, it would seem unreasonable to *assume* that the many factors which affect the growth rates would be the same in all cases. (The author hereby expresses his appreciation to Professors George Mulfinger and Ray Gsell for their assistance in interpreting these dripstone formations.)

them on the biblical teaching) elementary historical geology, into which then the geological data will have to fit![35]

In concluding his article, van de Fliert hammers home his main points:

> A fundamentalistic or biblicistic viewpoint ... implies the belief that the Bible teaches us principles, fundamentals or elements of human science in general and of historical-geological science in particular. For the fundamentalist, therefore, the reliability of the Bible as the Word of God is related to *scientific* reliability. For him this is particularly true of the first eleven chapters of Genesis. This conception, however, implies inevitably that science and God's revelation in the first chapters of the Bible are placed on the same (scientific) level, on the basis of which scientifically obtained data about the history of the earth and man will have to fit into the "Biblical scheme or framework."[36]

Let us pause to analyze these remarkable statements. If this is really a valid basis for approaching the early chapters of Genesis, it must also be valid for other historical sections of the Bible. What would happen if Christian *archaeologists* or Christian *historians* took this approach to Bible history? To help us in measuring the magnitude of this theological blunder, we will take van de Fliert's words and substitute (in italics) the term "history" for "historical geology" and the word "Exodus" for the word "Genesis."

> Any attempt to harmonize the *history* of today with the account of the first chapters of *Exodus* represents a misunderstanding of the *Exodus* record. . . . The Bible does not give outlines of *history* nor accounts of *historically* controllable creative acts of God! . . . Christians who do believe in God corrupt *historical* work thoroughly when they start from pretended biblical (in fact, imposed by them on the biblical teaching) elementary *history* into which then the *historical* data will have to fit! . . . This conception, however, implies inevitably that *history* and God's revelation in the first chapters of *Exodus* are placed on the same *historical* level, on the basis of which *historically* obtained data about the *history of Egypt and Israel* will have to fit into the "Biblical scheme or framework."

Would the *International Reformed Bulletin* or *Faith and*

35. van de Fliert, "Fundamentalism," p. 69.
36. van de Fliert, "Fundamentalism," p. 80.

Thought (Journal of the Victoria Institute) or even the *Journal of the American Scientific Affiliation,* which printed with approval van de Fliert's treatment of the early chapters of Genesis, be willing to publish the substituted words above with regard to the early chapters of Exodus? Presumably not, for they would at that very moment cease to be recognized as evangelical Christian publications and would lose the support of evangelical Christians.

But by what sleight-of-hand maneuver do we handle Exodus in one way and Genesis in another? They are *both* quoted as authoritative, historical documents by Christ and the apostles! They are *both* filled with the details of time and place and persons that characterize sober history! In a study of "The Literary Form of Genesis 1-11," Walter C. Kaiser, Jr., Professor of Old Testament at Trinity Evangelical Divinity School, observes that in the first eleven chapters of Genesis

> there are 64 geographical terms, 88 personal names, 48 generic names and at least 21 identifiable cultural items (such as gold, bdellium, onyx, brass, iron, gopher wood, bitumen, mortar, brick, stone, harp, pipe, cities, towers) in those opening chapters. The significance of this list may be seen by comparing it, for example, with "the paucity of references in the Koran. The single tenth chapter of Genesis has five times more geographical data of importance than the whole of the Koran." Every one of these items presents us with the possibility of establishing the reliability of our author. The content runs head on into a description of the real world rather than recounting events belonging to another world or level of reality.[37]

Agreeing with Edward J. Young's profound *Studies in Genesis One,*[38] Dr. Kaiser concludes:

> The decision is easy: Genesis 1-11 is prose and not poetry. The use of the *waw* consecutive with the verb to describe sequential acts, the frequent use of the direct object sign and the so-called relative pronoun, the stress on definitions, and the spreading out of these events in a sequential order indicates that *we are in prose and not in poetry.* Say what *we* will, the author plainly intends to be doing the same thing in these chapters that he is doing in chapters 12-50. If we

37. Chapter 4 in *New Perspectives on the Old Testament,* ed. by J. Barton Payne (Waco, Texas: Word, Inc., 1970), p. 59.
38. E. J. Young, *Studies in Genesis One* (Nutley, N.J.: Presbyterian & Reformed Pub. Co., 1964), p. 105.

want a sample of what the author's poetry, with its Hebrew parallelism and fixed pairs, would look like, Genesis 4:23-24 will serve as an illustration.[39]

Thus, Genesis 1-11 is *detailed, accurate, prose, authoritative history!* Nevertheless, Professor van de Fliert, along with a number of his colleagues at the Free University of Amsterdam, has been so deeply influenced by Barthian and existential thought patterns that much of Bible history has lost its real meaning.[40] To such men, Genesis and other portions of God's Word that speak of supernatural events no longer belong in the realm of *real history,* but are classified as "suprahistorical." When the semantic veil is fully removed we discover that "supra-historical" simply means *non-historical.*[41] In the words of Merle Meeter:

> Van de Fliert attempts to depreciate Scripture after the fashion of Bultmannian neo-orthodoxy and the neo-Barthianism of his countrymen T. Baarda, H. M. Kuitert, and J. L. Koole, which impugn the trustworthiness of the Biblical authors by a *sitz-im-leben* allegation of their relative ignorance (historically conditioned, it is averred) and consequently unavoidable error: "It cannot be denied [van de Fliert pontificates] and should not be denied that as a result of this development our (scientific) world picture (Weltbild) has obtained huge dimensions, both in time and space and has become entirely different from that of the authors of the Bible."[42]

With devastating logic and a masterful choice of terms, Meeter concludes his analysis of van de Fliert's statement:

> Such a pronouncement is not only parochial intellectual snobbery, but it exposes a humanistically preconditioned and

---

39. W. C. Kaiser, "The Literary Form of Genesis 1-11," pp. 59-60.
40. For documentation of the trend toward the Neo-orthodoxy in this former stronghold of Reformed orthodoxy in the Netherlands, see Geoffrey Thomas, "Contending for the Faith in the Netherlands," *Torch and Trumpet,* Oct., 1968, pp. 19-23, with bibliography; and Renze O. DeGroot, "Synod Faces 'New Theology' of Amsterdam," *Torch and Trumpet,* May, 1971, pp. 18-19. This journal is now entitled, *The Outlook* (4855 Starr St., S.E., Grand Rapids, Mich. 49506).
41. See Carl F. H. Henry, *Frontiers in Modern Theology* (Chicago: Moody Press, 1964) pp. 41-64; and Clark H. Pinnock, *Biblical Revelation* (Chicago: Moody Press, 1971), pp. 217-27.
42. Merle Meeter, "Geology in the Dark or in Bible Light?" *International Reformed Bulletin,* No. 38 (July, 1969), p. 28.

supercilious attitude toward the Holy Spirit guided writers of Scripture (and toward what they wrote) that ends in consequential denial of Biblical reliability. Thus, such an assertion is also an unwitting derogation of the one true and holy God Who speaks authoritatively to mankind in His Word; for on whatever the Bible speaks, it does so without the least error. But *we misread* because of our unbiblical preconceptions and because of our accommodationistic and, finally, apostate capitulation to the norms of naturalism in its several quasi-scientific contemporary guises.[43]

Professor van de Fliert assures us, however, that the Book of Genesis stands in no danger whatsoever, for "the reliability of the Word of God spoken in this world through His prophets and apostles is *beyond the reach of scientific control, because the Bible is not a scientific book. As such, it is not vulnerable to the results of science.*"[44] But if the Bible is beyond the reach of scientific control and is not vulnerable to the results of scientific (or historical) research, its concepts become as puerile and insipid as the adventures of ancient Babylonian deities or the theology of Hinduism. The Biblical doctrines of Creation and the Flood would also fall into Sir Karl Popper's famous definitions of "bad theories."

A theory which is not refutable by any conceivable event is non-scientific. Irrefutability is not a virtue of a theory (as people often think) but a vice. Every "good" scientific theory is a prohibition; it forbids certain things to happen. The more a theory forbids, the better it is. Confirmations should count only if they are the result of *risky predictions;* that is to say, if, unenlightened by the theory in question, we should have expected an event which was incompatible with the theory—an event which would have refuted the theory.[45]

This is the colossal blunder of Neo-orthodoxy and theological existentialism. In attempting to "rescue" the Word of God from all possible contamination by "elevating" it to a realm of *Heilsgeschichte* ("salvation history")—a realm of "eternity" where no historian, archaeologist, or scientist can possibly test its statements—existential theology has only suc-

---

43. Meeter, "Geology," p. 29.
44. van de Fliert, "Fundamentalism," p. 80.
45. Summarized from Karl R. Popper, *Conjectures and Refutations* (London: Routledge and Kegan, Paul, 1963) by Norman Macbeth, *Darwin Retried,* p. 99.

ceeded in rendering the Word of God totally *irrelevant, unknowable,* and therefore *meaningless.*[46]

Is this really the kind of help Christians need from Professor van de Fliert in order to gain a deeper understanding of the Book of Genesis? Does this not reveal all too clearly that a prolonged and intensive study of geological phenomena and geological theories does not in and of itself constitute one as a theological "workman that needeth not to be ashamed, handling aright the word of truth" (II Tim. 2:15)? And does not this demonstrate, once and for all, that *the only consistent way to deny the doctrine of a universal Flood is to deny that any real history is taught in Genesis?*

In fundamentalism van de Fliert sees an immature faith that must tie Scripture closely to science, and thus is guilty of "a colossal overestimation of science."[47] But these are strange words to come from the pen of this scientist, whose estimation of science is so exalted that he is able to consider it "an indirect exegetical tool" designed to "test the reliability of our ideas and conceptions about the Bible, the inspiration, and the historicity of the first chapters of Genesis"![48] In fact, "the results of human scientific and technical advances during the last centuries" constitute a kind of *"revelation"* that has brought us into a "scientific world picture (Weltbild)" that is "entirely different from that of the authors of the Bible."[49] *So science is the new revelation for modern man, and provides the essential exegetical tool for determining the reliability of Scripture!* Thus, in the words of one prominent theologian,

---

46. Although Christian faith is not *created* by empirical data, it nevertheless is *characterized* by historical events that literally cry out for objective investigation (cf. Acts 1:3; 26:26; I Cor. 15:5-8). Evolutionism, on the contrary, and even uniformitarianism, do not really qualify as scientific theories because there is no valid test that their advocates can imagine whereby one might prove their world view to be in error! "Fortunately this has now become widely recognized. Amongst scientists one can mention von Bertalanffy (1952, p. 89); Birch and Ehrlich (1967); Murray Eden; Ernst Mayr; Alex Fraser and Marcel Schutzenberger (in Moorhead and Kaplan, eds., 1967); and amongst philosophers Sir Karl Popper (1963); A. R. Manser (1965) and A. D. Barker (1968)." Arthur Jones, "The Dogma of Evolution," in *Faith and Thought* Vol. 98, Nos. 2 & 3 (1970), p. 32.
47. van de Fliert, "Fundamentalism," p. 80. See the challenge to this statement by R. E. D. Clark, "A Double Standard?" in *Faith and Thought* (Vol. 98, No. 1, Autumn 1970), pp. 43 ff.
48. van de Fliert, "Fundamentalism," p. 80.
49. van de Fliert, "Fundamentalism," p. 80.

When [J. R. van de Fliert] as a geologist begins to work with his human finite tools, considers the geologists' conclusions concerning the age of the earth, its formation, and the possibility of a world wide flood, *the Bible is tied to science!!* The Bible is made to say what that small human effort, called natural science, has produced.... The final outcome is that *natural science is given a magisterial voice.*[50]

So confident is Professor van de Fliert that science (especially geology) must be our only authoritative guide to the handling of Genesis that he has in effect put up signs about that first book of God's Word reading: "Theologian, go home!"

We see theologians enter this field, as Professor Whitcomb now does, as Professor Aalders did in Holland a few decades ago, and as so many before them have done since the end of the Middle Ages. But these "scientific" battles for an infallible Word of God have been lost right from the start. In constant retreat, the theologians have had to surrender every position they had once taken in this struggle. That's what the history of the warfare between science and theology should have made conclusively clear.[51]

Can our Dutch geologist be really serious at this point? Does he really mean to say that theologians have no right to assert the historicity of any miraculous events recorded on the pages of Holy Scripture? Then he has clearly joined the ranks of those existentialists who believe that Christ "arose from the dead" while denying that the tomb became empty!

Now if Christ is preached that he hath been raised from the dead, how say some among you that there is no resurrection from the dead? But if there is no resurrection of the dead, neither hath Christ been raised: and if Christ hath not been raised, then is our preaching vain, your faith is also vain (I Cor. 15:12-14).

This may be a popular view among existentialists, but it is

---

50. George Van Groningen (formerly Prof. of Old Testament, Reformed Theological College, Geelong, Victoria; now Prof. of Bible, Dordt College, Sioux Center, Ia.), "Interpretation of Genesis," *Journal of the Evangelical Theological Society,* Vol. 13, No. 4 (Fall, 1970), p. 210. H. Harold Hartzler, Executive Secretary of the American Scientific Affiliation, keenly observed: "It seems to me that (J. R. van de Fliert) exhibits that which I find in so many writers, that science is a god and that the Bible is a secondary book." Letter to the Editor, *JASA,* March, 1970, p. 30.
51. van de Fliert, "Fundamentalism," p. 80.

clearly anti-Christian, for a denial of the bodily resurrection of Christ as an historical event is a total denial of Christianity (cf. Rom. 10:9-10; 1:4).

If Professor van de Fliert should insist that he *does* accept the testimony of the four Gospels to the fact of the empty tomb, then by what hermeneutical shift of gears does he deny the miraculous events of Genesis, which the same four Gospels repeatedly confirm?

Evangelical Christians have long recognized that the Bible is not a "scientific textbook" in the pedantic sense of a compendium of detailed descriptions of all kinds of things and events. But it is most definitely a scientific textbook from another standpoint. It is an absolutely authoritative and infallible textbook on *the philosophy of science.*[52] It provides for man the necessary frame of reference apart from which true science in the ultimate sense would be an impossible enterprise. But even beyond this, the Bible provides for us an accurate and objective record of events that have enormous scientific implications from the standpoint of our total world-and-life view.

Henry M. Morris Answers J. R. van de Fliert

After the appearance of van de Fliert's critique of *The Genesis Flood* co-author Henry M. Morris responded with a letter to the editor:[53]

> I appreciate very much the attention devoted to our book by Professor van de Fliert since most professional geologists have ignored it. However, I regret that he allowed himself to resort to emotional language in his discussion ("incredible," "flagrant nonsense," "extremely dangerous," "pretended scientific value," etc.). One evidence that evolutionary uniformitarianism is a religion rather than a science is the fact that its advocates almost invariably react emotionally whenever a fellow scientist questions it.

---

52. Edward J. Young observed that "although Genesis does not purport to be a textbook of science, nevertheless, when it touches upon scientific subjects, it is accurate. Science has never discovered any facts which are in conflict with the statements of Genesis 1 . . . not for an instance can its accurate statements be regarded as out of harmony with true science." (*An Introduction to the Old Testament;* Grand Rapids: Wm. B. Eerdmans Pub. Co., 1949, p. 54). See also Henry M. Morris, "The Bible *Is* A Textbook of Science," Chapter XI in *Studies in the Bible and Science* (Nutley, N.J.: Presbyterian and Reformed Pub. Co., 1966).

53. Henry M. Morris, Letter to the Editor, *JASA,* March, 1970, pp. 36-37.

We agree completely with most of Professor van de Fliert's paper and are puzzled as to why so much that is in agreement with *The Genesis Flood* is included in a polemic against it. In many instances it seems to be that he is battling a straw man of his own preconception—like those evolutionists who forever are attacking the supposed creationist doctrine of fixity of species.

Thus we have always stressed the uniformity of natural law as a basic principle in science. Similarly we recognize abundant evidence of extensive earth movements in the past, including overthrusting, folding, and other remarkable tectonic features which we do not see occurring at present. As a hydrologist and hydraulics engineer, I certainly believe that the same basic principles of hydraulics operating at present were in effect when the ancient lands and rivers were eroded and the ancient sediments were deposited. Furthermore we recognize the value of the standard geologic column as a taxonomic device and the fact that strata usually occur in the accepted order and that paleontologic criteria of identification are generally valid.

But the point of the discussion in *The Genesis Flood* (and not discussed by Professor van de Fliert) is that there are a great number of exceptions to the usual order in which the supposed physical criteria of overthrusting, reworking, etc., are *not* present, and that there are a great many geologic features which (on consistent uniformitarian principles) could not possibly be correlated with geologic phenomena actually observed by modern geologists, either quantitatively or qualitatively (e.g., regional volcanic terrains, continental glaciation, mountain-building, peneplain formation, fossil graveyards, incised meanders, regional alluviation, submarine canyon formation, and many others.) It seems to many of us that such things as these absolutely demand catastrophism of some sort, though within the framework of uniform natural law.

In the decade since *The Genesis Flood* was written (though I do not mean to suggest any connection) a significant reaction of orthodox geologists has emerged against the older uniformitarianism, with an increasingly frank recognition that local or regional catastrophism is fundamental in geologic interpretation. I have discussed this trend to some extent in two other papers.[54] Of course there is still as much

54. Cf. Henry M. Morris, "Science Versus Scientism in Historical Geology," *Quarterly of the C.R.S.,* Vol. 2, Oct., 1965; and "Sedi-

RAPID FORMATION OF OIL DEPOSITS

Uniformitarians must believe that oil was formed gradually more than 25,000,000 years ago. But the great pressures in deep oil wells around the world would make this impossible. "Such high pressures require sudden deep burial. Moreover, to retain them for periods greater than 10,000 to 100,000 years is apparently impossible under the observed permeabilities [ability to permit leakage of fluids] of the oil reservoir and trap formations" (Melvin Cook, *Prehistory and Earth Models,* p. 341; cf. pp. 233-53). "It has now been experimentally demonstrated that cellulosic (plant derived) material, such as garbage or manure, can be converted into a good grade of petroleum in 20 minutes. . . . The experiments of Bureau of Mines scientists in which cow manure was converted to petroleum are described in *Chemical and Engineering News,* May 29, 1972, p. 14. The process could also utilize other cellulosic materials such as wood, bark . . . . The manure was heated at 716 degrees F, at 2000 to 5000 pounds per square inch for 20 minutes in the presence of carbon monoxide and steam. *The product was a heavy oil of excellent heating quality.* The yield was about three barrels of oil per ton of manure . . . . Protoplasm and chlorophyll are present in marine organisms. These components readily decompose, *so there should be no difficulty in getting the reaction started, even at relatively low temperatures, during the conversion of these organisms to gas and oil.* The heat generated by compression, the increase of temperature with depth, and the heat generated by friction of crustal thrusting caused by the tremendous cataclysmic burial and earth movements which occurred at the time of the Flood would have caused the temperature to rise sufficiently to initiate the exothermic reaction (heat is given off during this chemical reaction)." (Duane T. Gish, "Petroleum in Minutes, Coal in Hours," *Acts and Facts,* Vol. 1, No. 4.)

antipathy as ever to the idea of a worldwide cataclysm such as the Biblical Flood.

In the book we attempted, in an exploratory way, to see how the actual observed data of geology and other sciences could be harmonized with the Biblical record of the Flood. We repeatedly stressed in the book that our proposed geologic interpretations are tentative and subject to revision with further study and evaluation. However, the one point we insisted on was that *the basic Christian presupposition of the inerrancy and perspicuity of the Genesis record must be maintained.* If this is not done, then the remaining system may possibly be theistic, but it can be neither Biblical nor truly Christian.

Now it is this fundamental requirement which not only van de Fliert but all other critics of *The Genesis Flood* have studiously ignored. Critics invariably dwell on certain supposed flaws in our geological perspective (e.g., our alleged failure to recognize the real nature of the geologists' concept of uniformitarianism, the supposed impropriety of documenting our case with quotations from men who don't agree with it, and our alleged ignorance of the fact that there really are some examples of overthrusting, re-working of sediments, and faunal mixing and other phenomena whose *universal* applicability we questioned, etc.), but they always pass by the much more important and fundamental fact that *the written word of God unequivocally teaches that there was a world-destroying cataclysm in the days of Noah!*

This reaction of course is to be expected from non-Christian geologists, to whom the Biblical record is utterly irrelevant anyhow. But it is disheartening and puzzling when evangelical scientists, who insist that they still believe in the divine authority of the Bible, also completely ignore this powerful Biblical evidence for the world-wide cataclysm, as presented in *The Genesis Flood* and many other places. That this is a fair statement of the situation has been thoroughly confirmed in a recent study[55] by a man who has analyzed all the reviews and criticisms of *The Genesis Flood* since its initial publication.

Professor van de Fliert admits, in fact, that "our scien-

---

mentation and the Fossil Record: A Study in Hydraulic Engineering," *Quarterly of the C.R.S.,* Vol. 2, Dec., 1967.
55. Charles C. Clough, "A Calm Appraisal of *The Genesis Flood*" (unpublished Th.M. thesis, Dallas Theological Seminary, 1968). This study is summarized in the *Creation Research Quarterly* for September, 1969, pp. 81-84.

tific world picture has become different from that of the authors of the Bible."[56] To him, therefore, the fact the writer of Genesis (as well as Job, David, Isaiah, Paul, Peter, and even Christ Himself) believed in a global Flood is of no importance. He feels this issue can be settled simply by saying that "the Bible is not a scientific book." He even thinks (and one is almost startled to encounter this kind of circumlocution in a serious scientist and Christian) that to apply the Biblical doctrine of inerrancy to matters of historic fact is "a colossal overestimation of science."

Atheistic scientists and philosophers, on the other hand, reason much more directly. To them, if the Bible is unreliable when it deals with matters of human observation and experience (i.e., science and history)—as it does with great emphasis and frequency—then it is surely not worth trusting when it attempts to treat intangibles such as sin and salvation, heaven and hell—and God!

Available space for this communication does not allow for a rebuttal to Professor van de Fliert's criticism of our discussion of hydrodynamic sorting as a partial explanation for the lithologic and paleontologic divisions in the strata of a sedimentary exposure, or of the highly uncertain growth rates and subsequent histories of ancient coral reefs, or of other geological problems. I can only say that he has not at all settled these questions.

But this is not the important thing. I again acknowledge that there are many, many problems in geology for which we do not yet have adequate answers in terms of the Biblical framework, even though we can at least see in a general way how many of the data can be reinterpreted to correlate with it. There are even more serious problems, on the other hand, for the dogmatic evolutionist and uniformitarian.

The real crux of the matter, however, is "What saith Scripture?" In *The Genesis Flood,* as well as in our other writings, Dr. Whitcomb and I have maintained, with a considerable number of straightforward Biblical arguments, that the Bible teaches a recent special Creation of all things and a worldwide Flood, and that there is no permissible interpretation of the Bible which can accommodate evolution and the geological ages. *No one has answered these arguments to date.*

How, for one example, can we harmonize the concept of a billion years of random variation, struggle for existence, natural selection, evolutionary dead-ends and extinctions without number, disease, confusion, disorder, decay, slaugh-

---

56. van de Fliert, "Fundamentalism," p. 80.

ter and death; with the fact of a God of perfect wisdom, order, power, and grace—who could easily have created all things complete and perfect from the beginning (as He has revealed in His Word), but who according to the consistent evolutionist and uniformitarian, chose the tortuous route of evolution instead? This is a serious theological problem, one that cannot really be settled by a quip or a platitude.

It seems to me that each evangelical scientist and theologian owes it to the Christian community to do one of two things: (1) develop a sound Biblical exegesis of the fundamental chapters of the Bible (Genesis 1-11), consistent with the rest of Scripture, which will clearly warrant his acceptance of the geological ages and the general evolutionary world-view; or else (2) develop a re-interpretation of the observed facts of geology and other sciences to correlate with the facts of Biblical revelation concerning primeval earth history, centered in special Creation, the Fall, and the Flood.

There can be only confusion and danger in continuing to embellish the superstructure when the foundation has been destroyed.[57]

"Speak to the Earth, and It Shall Teach Thee"[58]

Let us now consider the extent to which the Bible provides for us *a philosophy of historical geology*—a God-given frame of reference apart from which the science of geology could never fulfill its legitimate goal of explaining *all* the kinds of forces that have affected and will yet affect the planet earth. Does an objective analysis of Bible history yield to us any concrete examples of geological phenomena which cannot be explained apart from a purely supernatural cause? Beginning with one famous episode recorded in all four Gospels, in which it will be our purpose to discover a fundamental theological principle, we shall then move to various Old Testament passages that illustrate and amplify this principle.

Who Moved the Stone?[59]

The four Gospels give us considerable detail concerning the most famous stone in history—the stone that blocked the entrance to the tomb of the Lord Jesus Christ. Matthew reports that Joseph of Arimathea rolled "a great stone" (Mark

---

57. Henry M. Morris, Letter to the Editor, *JASA,* March, 1970, pp. 36-37.
58. Job 12:8.
59. This is the title of a famous apologetic for the resurrection of Christ by Frank Morison (London: Faber and Faber Ltd., first published in 1930, reprinted in 1969).

says "an exceeding great" stone—16:4) against the tomb, and that the stone was sealed to the tomb by Jewish and Roman authorities to prevent any of the disciples of Jesus from stealing the body (Matt. 27:57-66). There it stood, having been positioned by human plans and energies and now firmly fixed by gravitational and governmental decree.

But what happened to this great stone? All true Christians know. During the night, "an angel of the Lord descended from heaven, and came and rolled away the stone" (Matt. 28:2).[60] We are now confronted squarely by the ultimate question: was this a scientific/historic event that occurred in the vicinity of Jerusalem about nineteen centuries ago?

This very question was put to Professor van de Fliert by a professor of history at East Carolina University who was disturbed by the Dutch geologist's method of separating science from the Bible by use of "a Kantian dialectic wherein science is restricted to a purely physical, phenomenal realm. The difficulty then arises in such Biblical events as the rolling away from the door of Christ's tomb of the immense boulder by an angel. Here we are presented with a direct intervention into the physical, phenomenal sphere, *even the geological sphere,* of a supernatural activity. How are we to understand this narrative?"[61]

Professor van de Fliert's answer to this highly relevant and straightforward question is filled with uncertain sounds:

> I fear speculation, particularly when the Bible is concerned. I can speak scientifically about fossils and sedimentary layers in the earth crust, documents within the field of my scientific experience. By what means could we pretend to speak adequately, scientifically, on what exactly happened at Jesus' resurrection? It is beyond the field of our scientific experience as far as I know and so long as that is the case I want to have the right to say to an inquisitive man: I don't know! . . . On things like these I can only speak as the Bible speaks about God's unique work, in human language, in the common prescientific parlance. . . .[62]

Is this the way early Christians would have answered this ques-

---

60. The stone was not removed to let Jesus get out (cf. John 20:19, 26), but rather to let the disciples get in (cf. John 20:1-13).

61. William White, Jr., "The Fundamentals of Fundamentalism and Geology," *International Reformed Bulletin,* No. 38 (July, 1969), p. 30. (Italics added.)

62. J. R. van de Fliert, "Bible, Man and Science: A Reply," *International Reformed Bulletin,* No. 38 (July, 1969), p. 37.

tion? Were there any uncertain "Kantian" sounds in the apostle Paul's proclamation of this historical/geological/theological event? "Ye are saved, if ye hold fast the word which I preached unto you, except ye believed in vain. For I delivered unto you first of all that which also I received . . . that he hath been raised on the third day according to the scriptures . . ." (I Cor. 15:2-4); and the very Scripture already quoted above has much to say about the movement of that stone.

If, as orthodox Christians have believed from the beginning of the Church, the Gospels give us an infallible record of events in the time of Christ, then the movement of that stone must have geological as well as theological implications. It must mean that geologic uniformitarianism, at least at that point, has suffered a shattering blow as a completely consistent and ultimately satisfying world view. It serves as a clear example of how one solid exception can upset an otherwise impressive "law" of the universe.

Thus, to the extent that a uniformitarian philosophy of geology makes it impossible for one to believe that a large stone could have been moved by purely angelic/divine power, then to that same extent it is impossible for a true Christian to be a uniformitarian geologist. Why? Because (1) no one can deny the bodily resurrection of Christ in history and be a true Christian (cf. Rom. 10:9), and (2) the only records we have of the bodily resurrection of Christ all explain the movement of the stone as an important evidence of Christ's resurrection.

Therefore, it is the limits of God's written Word, not merely "the limits of their own scientific field" that geologists must honor if they are to be counted among those who are God's people. Christian geologists, like all other Christians, must fear God and submit to His Word. They are not exempt from the promise of our Lord, "ye shall know the truth, and the truth shall make you free;" but this can only be true because they are also not exempt from the words that precede and condition this great promise: "If ye abide in my word, then are ye truly my disciples" (John 8:31).

"Great Stones From Heaven"[63]

Not long after Israel crossed the Jordan, the Canaanite armies of southern Palestine challenged the invaders and were utterly routed by God's direct intervention. "And it came to pass, as they fled from before Israel, while they were at the descent of Beth-horon, that Jehovah cast down *great stones*

---

63. Joshua 10:11.

from heaven upon them unto Azekah, and they died: they were more who died with the hailstones than they whom the children of Israel slew with the sword" (Josh. 10:11). The five Canaanite kings fled and hid themselves in a cave at Makkedah. "And Joshua said, Roll *great stones* [same Hebrew words as in verse 11] unto the mouth of the cave" (Josh. 10:18).

Whether these "great stones from heaven" consisted of rocky or of metallic substance is not of importance to us. The important point, from the perspective of an adequate world-view that encompasses *all* significant geological events is that these thousands of stones were flung from heaven in such a way that fleeing Canaanites were killed by them but pursuing Israelites were not. And the fact that we cannot distinguish those particular stones along the descent of Beth-horon today is likewise irrelevant to the major issue. The important fact is that thousands of men died from the impact of these astronomic/geologic missiles, and they were available for close study by the Israelites who saw them fall before their very eyes. Uniformitarian geology, however useful it may be in explaining many of the earth's geological phenomena, would be of no help whatsoever in explaining those "great stones from heaven."

Geologic Miracles in the Wilderness

Moving back beyond the military campaigns of Joshua in Canaan to the days of Moses' leadership in the wilderness wanderings, we find two episodes of special geological significance.

Twice over Moses with his rod struck the rock, once at the command of God and the other time in ire; and in each instance the rock split and the waters gushed out. The fractures this produced in the earth's crust also constituted for Israel memorials to the gracious provision of God, *and no geologist could give a true explanation of them without the the light of God's Word*. And the ugly scar likely left where the earth broke open and swallowed up the families of Korah, Dathan, and Abiram remained a memorial to divine justice carried out over the wickedness of these rebels; *and geologists would again have to consult the Scriptures for a true meaning of this irregularity in the earth's crust*.[64]

---

64. Ring Star, "Geological Science and Biblical Data," *The Banner*, September 25, 1970, p. 4. (Italics added.) These events are described in Numbers 20:10-11 and 16:28-34.

The power of this Biblical evidence for supernatural causes behind certain geologic effects in history abides in exact proportion to the seriousness with which the Scriptural testimony is accepted by modern minds and hearts. The events *did* happen within the continuum of time and space, but no one can point to the visible effects in the Sinai region today.

The Destruction of Sodom and Gomorrah[65]

Moving yet closer to the time of the Flood, we ponder an even more spectacular divine intervention from the standpoint of historical geology. If we cannot find the tombstone of Jesus in the place to which it was moved; if we can no longer identify the great stones from heaven; if we cannot locate the split rock and the split crust in the Wilderness, we *can* see the effects of God's judgment upon the five Cities of the Plain:

> It must certainly be emphasized at the outset that, whatever may have caused the calamity, something surely happened at the south. end of the Dead Sea which was of an extraordinary character. No ordinary conflagration occurred, but a catastrophe so great and so awful, that the memory of it remained fixed in men's minds and the story of it was passed down by word of mouth for centuries before the biblical narratives were written.[66]

But can we really be certain that the shallow southern extension of the Dead Sea is the area where those notoriously wicked cities were located? J. Penrose Harland concludes his careful analysis with these words:

> In summary, one may conclude that the evidence from the Bible and from the late Greek and Latin writers indicates a location around the southern end of the Sea. And this localization is supported by other evidence derived from geology, hydrography (study of water supply), and from both positive and negative results of archaeological investigations.[67]

Theologians and Scientists

Are the passages cited above from the books of Genesis, Numbers, Joshua, Matthew, Mark, Luke, and John to be

---

65. See Genesis 19:24-29; Isaiah 1:9, 13:19; Jeremiah 20:16, 49:18; Amos 4:11; Zephaniah 2:9; Luke 17:29, 32; II Peter 2:6; Jude 7.
66. J. Penrose Harland, "Sodom and Gomorrah," in *The Biblical Archaeologist Reader,* ed. by G. Ernest Wright and David Noel Freedman (New York: Anchor Books, Doubleday & Co., 1961), p. 59.
67. Harland, "Sodom and Gomorrah," p. 47.

taken seriously when they tell us that God has supernaturally intervened at definite times and places to destroy cities, split the earth's crust, hurtle stones at fleeing armies, and move a huge boulder from the tomb of Jesus?

If the living God not only *can,* but actually *has* intervened in such spectacular ways, producing tangible and visible geologic effects, then why could He not also break up the fountains of the great deep and release the upper waters to bring upon the earth a universal Flood? And if it is legitimate to search for the geologic effects of His destruction of Sodom and Gomorrah at the southern neck of the Dead Sea, why may we not search for effects of the world-wide Deluge in the vast sedimentary deposits of our world? Is not this exactly what one would expect to find from such a uniquely destructive, year-long aqueous catastrophe, according to all known laws of hydrodynamics?

In the minds of many Christian geologists, however, this is not only an illegitimate enterprise but a very dangerous one. Professor van de Fliert reads about such efforts "with increasing astonishment." In fact, such efforts are to him "incredible" and "extremely dangerous," constituting "a death-blow to the Christian religion," causing Christians to "lose the Bible as a reliable Word of God completely." Such an approach to earth history "tends to transform twentieth-century Christians into aliens" and "tends to deprive them of their belief in a reliable Bible," actually alienating them "from the Words of Eternal Life."[68]

Another Christian geologist, Roger J. Cuffey, denounces those who are trying to give scientific prominence to the Flood as being "ignorant of modern earth science" and therefore "pseudo-scientific." He writes of the "stunned disbelief that so many of us have had when we have seen how the flood-geologists, instead of being properly laughed out of court, were widely accepted in the intelligent Christian community. This, incidentally, is leading many geologists, both Christian and non-Christian, to think that our general-science-type courses have been total failures if the average college-educated person can't recognize as big a blunder as this one when he encounters it."[69]

Walter R. Hearn, book review editor for the *Journal of the American Scientific Affiliation,* could not imagine anyone having the temerity to challenge "the house of geological

68. van de Fliert, "Fundamentalism," pp. 69, 80.
69. Roger J. Cuffey, comment on J. R. van de Fliert, "Fundamentalism," in *JASA,* Sept., 1969, p. 71.

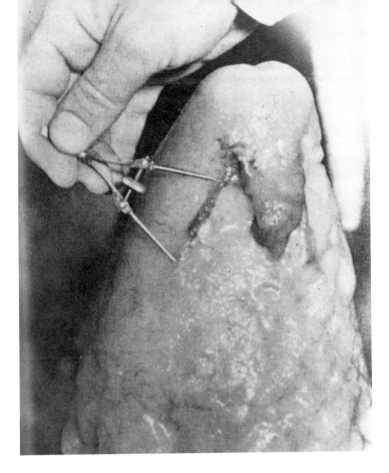

A BAT INSIDE A STALAGMITE AT CARLSBAD CAVERNS

The fact that a bat could be cemented inside a stalagmite (Carlsbad Caverns, New Mexico) supplies an important clue to the problem of stalagmite growth rate. Uniformitarians are in serious error when they assert that stalagmite accretion requires multiple thousands of years. Evidently it sometimes occurs so rapidly that a bat can be entombed before action of bacterial decay and/or predators. Thus the growth of dripstone formations can (under certain conditions) be described as *catastrophic.*

This photograph was first published in *National Geographic Magazine*, October, 1953, p. 442, in an article by Mason Sutherland, "Carlsbad Caverns in Color." A review of this article by Robert Harris has been published in the *Creation Research Society Quarterly*, September, 1971, p. 144.

science" which "those who dwell inside ... have been in the process of remodeling continuously ever since it was built," and replacing this magnificent structure of evolutionary uniformitarianism with "the fine new edifice" which "the pages of the family Bible" lay out for us.[70]

Frank H. Roberts felt that "most geologists would be amazed to learn" of such efforts;[71] and Wayne U. Ault asserted that "as far as the scientific secular world is concerned, *The Genesis Flood* will likely pass quite unnoticed. At most it may be taken as a poignant example of someone from another discipline attempting to plunge into the multiple disciplines of geological science and come up with a new scheme that agrees with certain select preconceptions [such as those of Christ and the Apostles?]. On the evangelical Christian world the book, regrettably, may have more of an impact; it could lead to the unfortunate result of retarding the development of true Christian scholarship in the younger generation."[72]

When Delbert N. Eggenberger retired from the editorship of the A.S.A. Journal in 1962, he penned these words: "Some subjects were active in the earlier years but have waned because they were pretty well threshed out at conventions and in papers. Editorial selection prevented later duplication of the same material. *An example of this is flood geology.*"[73] But the vital topic refused to be suppressed. By 1965 another editor appealed to his readers: "Dying embers of *The Genesis Flood* are still around. Another criticism of previous criticisms has been received by the editor. Do you want it or have you had enough?"[74]

Apparently readers of the Journal had not had enough. Somewhat in desperation, Richard H. Bube, who became editor in 1968, asked: "Will the A.S.A. break clear of the dry bones of arguments about creation, evolution, Adam, and the flood, and combine scientific insight with the Gospel of Jesus Christ to speak to the problems that concern today's world?"[75] It was presumably for the purpose of implementing

---

70. Walter R. Hearn, editorial for "Book Reviews," *JASA,* March, 1964, p. 28.
71. Frank H. Roberts, review of *The Genesis Flood,* in *JASA,* March, 1964, p. 28.
72. Wayne U. Ault, review of *The Genesis Flood,* in *JASA,* March, 1964, p. 31.
73. Delbert N. Eggenberger, "The ASA Periodical: The First One and One-Half Decades," *JASA,* March, 1963, p. 4. (Italics added.)
74. Marlin Kreider, "Book Reviews," *JASA,* March, 1965, p. 30.
75. Richard H. Bube, "The President Speaks," *JASA,* March, 1968,

this goal that Dr. Bube sponsored the reprinting of Professor van de Fliert's article "Fundamentalism and the Fundamentals of Geology" the following year. Surely the "dry bones of arguments about creation, evolution, Adam, and the flood" would at last be buried, once and for all.

But such was not to be the case, as subsequent issues of the *Journal of the American Scientific Affiliation* make abundantly clear. Paul H. Seely, a prominent scientist in the ranks of the A.S.A. cried out in desperation:

> The Whitcomb and Morris delusion, mythology, or whatever one wishes to call such a well-meant, but ill-devised pseudo-science has captured literally hundreds of Christian high schools, Bible schools, and seminaries . . . and through the graduates of these schools, the minds of thousands of Christians. It spreads like a giant cancer . . . unfelt by the Church for a time, but in the end . . . making its obscurantism result in disillusionment, debacle, and spiritual death.[76]

Pondering the great storm of emotional reactions which this issue was creating among scientists in the A.S.A., a Harvard graduate challenged the editors of the Journal:

> The ASA *may* be lapsing into a party line—theistic evolution. I realize that since the break-off of the Creation Research people, you are more or less inclined to debunk flood geology, etc., but I do hope that as *Christians* you will not close your minds to truth. . . . Van de Fliert's attitude toward the flood theory and its proponents is, to say the least, haughty in its assumed omniscience. Van de Fliert *presupposes* the absolute truth in his position in order to discredit the other! Thus his "disproof" consists in spewing back contemporary uniformitarian assumptions and "facts"—it is *unthinkable* ostensibly for him to even consider any other

p. 2. In his presidential newsletter to all members of the A.S.A., November-December, 1968, Dr. Bube quoted an anonymous writer: "My direct observation of the rapid advance of the 'young earth' doctrine has convinced me that this is an alarming problem among evangelical Christians today. The advocates of this doctrine are in many cases very fine Christian gentlemen whom I respect, but the fact that they are converting people to their way of thinking so much faster than we are frightens me." He appealed to the A.S.A. for helpful arguments, because up to the present "we are not providing much." Dr. Bube responded with the hope that in the future a "conscientious analysis of the scientific data" might be forthcoming.

76. Paul H. Seely, "Adam and Anthropology," *JASA,* March, 1971, p. 26.

hypothesis. This is not Christian thinking. ... I must say that I, having studied this issue with some diligence, ... see tremendous possibilities in this Flood theory.[77]

In the meantime, one prominent scientist-theologian in the American Scientific Affiliation vigorously protested against this degrading of Genesis on the part of some of his fellow evangelical scientists:

> I am appalled at the freedom with which our Christian scientists are toying with the Biblical texts. I may soften that by adding that our theologians are doing so too and so the scientists naturally are taking it up. But the scientists should have a chance to hear the criticisms of various theologians rather than jumping to the first far out exegesis of Genesis that seems to meet the scientific need.[78]

From Australia came this appeal by two widely recognized Reformed theologians who were well acquainted with the writings of J. R. van de Fliert, Jan Lever, and other Christian scientists at the Free University of Amsterdam:

> We would plead with our scientist fellow Christians increasingly to give serious attention to what the theologians, who have a lifetime calling to study the revealed inscripturated Word, have to say on the subject of origins, creation, or evolution. We theologians will continue to read what the scientists are saying.[79]

But instead of entering into a more serious study of the actual statements of Scripture, or even an objective reappraisal of the presuppositions underlying their own interpretations of the geologic phenomena (e.g., the Grand Canyon formations), some A.S.A. scientists found it easier to utter the traditional defensive cry: "Galileo is being persecuted again!"[80] This would supposedly ward off further inter-

---

77. John M. Batteau, "Tone Down the Rhetoric," *JASA,* June, 1972, p. 75.
78. R. Laird Harris, Letter to the Editor, *JASA,* December, 1964, p. 127.
79. Klaas Runia and George Van Groningen, Reply to "Thinking Cap—Or Night Cap?" by Peter G. Berkhout, in *The Banner,* March 5, 1965, p. 24. See also, George Van Groningen, "Genesis: Its Formation and Interpretation," in *Interpreting God's Word Today,* ed. by Simon Kistemaker (Grand Rapids: Baker Book House, 1970), pp. 30-34.
80. For example, Peter G. Berkhout, "The Bible of Nature," *JASA,* Dec., 1967, p. 112. Charles E. Hummel wisely comments: "Galileo is pictured as a brave martyr suffering the persecution of re-

the basic issue: is the Bible truly God's Word? • 137

ference from conservative Old Testament scholars and theologians who were becoming appalled by the irresponsible handling of Scripture within A.S.A. leadership.

> What we are faced with is a kind of trial of Galileo in reverse. The (theologians) are saying: "We have questions that may undermine some of your scientific dogmas," and the "scientific" party is in effect replying: "Your objections are not scientific and may under no circumstances be permitted to threaten the confidence of the (constituency) in our teachings."[81]

But the "Galileo" watchword seemed somewhat hollow when it was observed that the minority of scientists in the A.S.A. who still took Genesis seriously were effectively bypassed by the Journal editors and therefore found it necessary to launch a new organization in 1963 called the Creation Research Society with a membership (restricted to scientists) that soon mounted to hundreds.[82]

Conclusion

The powerful grip that uniformitarianism has gained upon the minds of many Christian men of science may be measured, in part, by the violent reaction that has come from the American Scientific Affiliation to all serious efforts to challenge this philosophy at its very roots. The fact that this challenge has come from the twin perspectives of careful exegesis of Scripture and responsible handling of the scientific data has forced Christian uniformitarians to respond, all too often, with appeals to scientific "authority" and traditional scientific

---

ligious dogmatism. But this version, which enjoys widespread popularity, is actually a rationalist myth which grew up in the last century. Historical research has shown that Galileo's conflict was not with Biblical revelation but with Aristotelian natural philosophy defended by scholasticism" ("The Scientific Revolution of the 16th and 17th Centuries," *JASA,* Dec., 1968, p. 101). For an excellent analysis of what actually happened to Galileo, see Jerome J. Langford, *Galileo, Science and the Church,* (rev. ed.; Ann Arbor: The University of Michigan Press, 1971), pp. 1-158.

81. Adapted from Harold Lindsell's critique of the modern scientific establishment in its resistance to creationism being tolerated in public schools. Editorial, *Christianity Today,* Jan. 5, 1973, p. 354.

82. At the time of this split, the A.S.A. had fewer than one thousand members. Later, a theistic evolutionist in the A.S.A. commented somewhat sanguinely: "[Creation Research Society people] are well-meaning Christians; but to me they appear as a remnant of a passing race" (Peter G. Berkhout, "The Bible of Nature," *JASA,* Dec., 1967, p. 112). For a list of some recent C.R.S. publications, see above, p. 64, Note 35.

clichés. Some geologists, especially Professor J. R. van de Fliert of the Free University of Amsterdam, have sought to relieve the tension by dissolving the early chapters of Genesis into a meaningless, existential "suprahistory."

But the Book of Genesis cannot be dismissed so easily. As the foundational book of the inscripturated Word of God, it partakes of the inerrancy and infallibility that our Lord Jesus Christ attributed to the entire Bible. And, like some other books of the Bible, it contributes to a "Biblical philosophy of geology" which provides the necessary frame of reference for a totally satisfying approach to historical geology. Only if we possess this divinely revealed philosophy of geology can we work out the details of a *total system* in accordance with God's command to Adam and to the entire human race: "... fill the earth, and *subdue* it ..." (Gen. 1:28, NASB).

summary

Why do sincere and scholarly Christians differ so greatly on the Biblical doctrine of the Flood? It is not because of any lack of Biblical or even scientific evidence, but because of different starting points. If one *begins* with the complex array of scientific data and current interpretations of these data without a revealed and thus infallible frame of reference, the conclusions will be ultimately self-contradictory. But with God's Word as his guiding light, one can look at the scientific data from a unifying perspective and thus be assured of ultimate satisfaction.

Many Christian men of science have erred in their interpretation of earth history because of a serious lack of Biblical perspective. Deeply perplexed by the enormous mass of scientific data—strata, fossils, varves, craters, glaciers, mountains, evaporites, canyons, deltas, stalagmites—all interpreted for them since childhood in uniformitarian and evolutionary terms, they have neglected God's Word as the divinely given guide to earth history. They have somehow felt that the early chapters of Genesis are true, but only in a vaguely "religious" sense, especially in those areas that overlap the supposed domain of the historical sciences.

But this underestimation of the historical relevance of Scripture has led to both theological and scientific disaster. The Biblical doctrine of Creation has been hopelessly compromised, and the great Flood has been reduced to a mere river flood in Mesopotamia. This, in turn, has opened the door to such drastic heresies as neo-orthodoxy and theological existentialism, which know no consistent stopping point short of a complete abandonment of the Bible as God's Word and of God as a personal being.

But all of this can and must be avoided. Our Lord Jesus Christ stated the basic principle quite clearly: "Whosoever shall not receive the kingdom of God as a little child, he shall in no wise enter therein" (Mark 10:15). This is certainly not intended by our Lord to put a premium upon ignorance. Rather, it places the premium upon an attitude of openness of heart to the final authority of God's Word. Nothing can be as important in the human/divine relationship as that. Speaking of man's best achievements in the realm

THE SHORELINE OF SURTSEY ISLAND

Bursting out of the Atlantic Ocean a few miles south of Iceland in 1963, the new island of Surtsey represents yet another challenge to uniformitarians. Within a matter of months, "surging surf ground jagged lava into rounded boulders with a speed that astonished geologists attending Surtsey's birth" (Samuel W. Matthews, "This Changing Earth," *National Geographic Magazine*, Jan., 1973, p. 5).

The Icelandic geologist Sigurdur Thorarinsson observed: "On Surtsey, only *a few months* have sufficed for a *landscape to be created* which is *so varied and mature* that it is *almost beyond belief.* Here we not only have a lava dome with a glowing lava lake in a summit crater and red-hot lava-flows rushing down the slopes, increasing the height of the dome and transforming the configuration of the island from one day to another. Here we can also see wide sandy beaches and precipitous crags lashed by breakers of the sea. There are gravel banks and lagoons, impressive tephra (basaltic ash) cliffs, greyish-white from the brine and silicium which oozes out of the tephra, giving them a resemblance to the White Cliffs on the English Channel. There are hollows, glens and soft undulating land. There are fractures and faultscarps, channels and screes . . . . You may come to a beach covered with flowing lava on its way to the sea . . . . *Three weeks later you may come back to the same place and be literally confounded by what meets your eye.* Now there are precipitous lava cliffs of considerable height, and below them you will see boulders worn by the surf, some of which are almost round, on an abrasion platform cut into the cliff, and further out there is a sandy beach where you can walk at low tide without getting wet" (*Surtsey: The New Island in the North Atlantic,* Reykjavik, Iceland: Almenna Bokafelagio, 1964, p. 52. Italics added. Quoted by Wilbert H. Rusch in *Why Not Creation?* ed. by Walter E. Lammerts, Nutley, N.J.: Presbyterian and Reformed Publishing Co., 1970, p. 139).

of religion, the apostle Paul asks, "Hath not God made foolish the wisdom of the world?" (I Cor. 1:20). Foolishness—in the Biblical sense of that term—is a willful refusal to accept God's explanations of reality in favor of mere human explanations.

Uniformitarian geologists today are far less rigid than their nineteenth-century counterparts. They speak of their new freedom and flexibility, even to the point of tolerating major catastrophes. But the trend is somewhat dangerous for their uniformitarian/evolutionary model of earth history. Can their system absorb the discovery that the earth's magnetic field began less than 15,000 years ago because of its present rate of dissipation? Or the lack of helium in the atmosphere in spite of rapid accretion through radioactive decay processes? Or the lack of meteoritic dust on the moon and earth in spite of its present rapid rate of accumulation? Or the discovery that oil reservoirs are of recent origin because of the impossibility of long maintaining high fluid pressures under the observed permeabilities of reservoir and trap formations? Or the necessarily sudden and recent formation of all of the earth's vast coal deposits? Or the rapid formation and excavation of the Grand Canyon, together with the presence of pollen grains in its lowest strata? Or the presence of human footprints in the same rock layers with the footprints of huge reptilian dinosaurs? If Christian geologists who have been deeply influenced by the uniformitarian philosophy of earth history ignore such discoveries, does this not raise legitimate questions concerning their sense of fairness and objectivity, to say nothing of their submission to God's Word?

Biblical catastrophists do not claim that any particular geologic phenomenon in and of itself demonstrates the universal Flood. Scientific empiricism was never intended by God to be the direct and essential link to Biblical revelation. To the contrary, Scripture has been given to provide us with the light we need for understanding the origin and meaning of our geologic environment. To this extent, at least, the Christian is committed to a form of deductive reasoning. "For with thee is the fountain of life: In thy light shall we see light" (Ps. 36:9). The geologic data, at best, serve as *circumstantial evidences* for the reality of the Genesis Flood. But the *ultimate basis* for our confidence in its reality consists of the direct statements of our Lord Jesus Christ and His apostles, to the effect that "the world that then was, being overflowed with water, perished."

bibliography

Archer, Gleason L., Jr. *A Survey of Old Testament Introduction.* Chicago: Moody Press, 1964.

Ault, Wayne U. Review of *The Genesis Flood,* by John C. Whitcomb, Jr., and Henry M. Morris. *Journal of the American Scientific Affiliation.* XVI:1 (March, 1964), 29-31.

Cansdale, George S. "A Universal Flood: Some Practical Difficulties." *Faith and Thought,* XCVIII:2, 3 (1970), 61-68.

Clark, R. T., and Bales, J. D. *Why Scientists Accept Evolution.* Nutley, N.J.: Presbyterian and Reformed Pub. Co., 1966.

Clementson, Sidney P. "A Critical Examination of Radioactive Dating of Rocks." *Creation Research Society Quarterly,* VII (December, 1970), 137-41.

Clough, Charles A. "A Calm Appraisal of *The Genesis Flood.*" Unpublished Th.M. thesis, Dallas Theological Seminary, 1968.

————. *Laying the Foundation.* Lubbock, Texas: Lubbock Bible Church, 1973.

Cook, Melvin A. *Prehistory and Earth Models.* London: Max Parrish and Co., 1966.

Custance, Arthur C. *The Extent of the Flood.* Doorway Papers, No. 41. Brockville, Ontario: By the Author, Box 291, 1958.

————. "Fossil Man in the Light of the Record in Genesis." *Why Not Creation?* Edited by Walter Lammerts. Nutley, N.J.: Presbyterian and Reformed Pub. Co., 1970.

Davidheiser, Bolton. *Evolution and Christian Faith.* Nutley, N.J.: Presbyterian and Reformed Pub. Co., 1969.

Filby, Frederick A. *The Flood Reconsidered.* Grand Rapids: Zondervan Pub. House, 1971.

Gish, Duane T. *Evolution: The Fossils Say No!* San Diego: Institute for Creation Research, 1972.

————. Speculations and Experiments Related to Theories on the Origin of Life. San Diego: Institute for Creative Research, 1972.

Harris, R. Laird. *Man—God's Eternal Creation.* Chicago: Moody Press, 1971.

————. "The Mist, the Canopy, and the Rivers of Eden."

Bulletin of the Evangelical Theological Society, XI:4 (Fall, 1968), 177-79.

Heidel, Alexander. *The Gilgamesh Epic and Old Testament Parallels.* 2nd ed. Chicago: University of Chicago Press, 1949.

Hooykaas, R. *The Principle of Uniformity in Geology, Biology and Theology.* Leiden: E. J. Brill, 1963.

Kaiser, Walter C., Jr. "The Literary Form of Genesis 1-11." *New Perspectives on the Old Testament.* Edited by J. Barton Payne. Waco, Texas: Word, Inc., 1970.

Kerkut, G. A. *Implications of Evolution.* New York: Pergamon Press, 1960.

Kidner, Derek. *Genesis: An Introduction and Commentary.* Chicago: Inter-Varsity Press, 1967.

Klotz, John W. *Genes, Genesis and Evolution.* St. Louis: Concordia Pub. House, 1955.

Lammerts, Walter, ed. *Scientific Studies in Special Creation.* Nutley, N.J.: Presbyterian and Reformed Pub. Co., 1971.

———, ed. *Why Not Creation?* Nutley, N.J.: Presbyterian and Reformed Pub. Co., 1970.

LaSor, William Sanford. Review of *The Genesis Flood,* by John C. Whitcomb, Jr., and Henry M. Morris. *Eternity,* XII:8 (August, 1961), 43.

Leupold, H. C. *Exposition of Genesis.* Grand Rapids: Baker Book House, 1942.

Macbeth, Norman. *Darwin Retried.* Boston: Gambit, Inc., 1971.

Meeter, Merle. "Geology in the Dark or in Bible Light?" *International Reformed Bulletin,* XXXVIII (July, 1969), 27-29.

Montgomery, John Warwick. *The Quest for Noah's Ark.* Minneapolis: Bethany Fellowship, Inc., 1972.

Moore, John N., and Slusher, Harold Schultz, eds. *Biology: A Search for Order in Complexity.* Grand Rapids: Zondervan Pub. House, 1970.

Morris, Henry M. "The Ark of Noah." *Creation Research Society Quarterly,* VIII:2 (September, 1971), 142-44.

———. *Biblical Cosmology and Modern Science.* Grand Rapids: Baker Book House, 1970.

———. Letter to the Editor. *Journal of the American Scientific Affiliation,* XXII:1 (March, 1970), 36-37.

———. *The Remarkable Birth of the Planet Earth.* San Diego: Institute for Creation Research, 1972.

———. *Studies in the Bible and Science.* Nutley, N.J.: Presbyterian and Reformed Pub. Co., 1966.

Morris, Henry M., and Wiggert, James M. *Applied Hydraulics in Engineering.* 2nd ed. New York: Ronald Press, 1972.

Patten, Donald W. *The Biblical Flood and the Ice Epoch.* Seattle: Pacific Meridian Pub. Co., 1966.

Ramm, Bernard. *The Christian View of Science and Scripture.* Grand Rapids: Wm. B. Eerdmans Pub. Co., 1954.

Roberts, Frank H. Review of *The Genesis Flood,* by John C. Whitcomb, Jr., and Henry M. Morris. *Journal of the American Scientific Affiliation,* XVI:1 (March, 1964), 28, 29.

Rupke, N. A. "Prolegomena to a Study of Cataclysmal Sedimentation." *Why Not Creation?* Edited by Walter E. Lammerts. Nutley, N.J.: Presbyterian and Reformed Pub. Co., 1970.

Schaeffer, Francis A. *Genesis in Space and Time.* Downers Grove, Ill.: Inter-Varsity Press, 1972.

van de Fliert, J. R. "Bible, Man and Science: A Reply." *International Reformed Bulletin,* XXXVIII (July, 1969), 34-39.

———. "Fundamentalism and the Fundamentals of Geology." *Journal of the American Scientific Affiliation,* XXI:3 (September, 1969), 69-81.

Velikovsky, Immanuel. *Earth in Upheaval.* New York: Dell Pub. Co., reprinted 1965.

Whitcomb, John C., Jr. *The Early Earth.* Grand Rapids: Baker Book House, 1972.

Whitcomb, John C., Jr., and Morris, Henry M. *The Genesis Flood.* Nutley, N.J.: Presbyterian and Reformed Pub. Co., 1961.

White, William, Jr. "The Fundamentals of Fundamentalism and Geology." *International Reformed Bulletin,* XXXVIII (July, 1969), 30-33.

Wilder Smith, A. E. *The Creation of Life.* Wheaton, Ill.: Harold Shaw Pub., 1970.

———. *Man's Origin, Man's Destiny.* Wheaton, Ill.: Harold Shaw Pub. Co., 1968.

Young, Davis A. Review of *The Encounter Between Christianity and Science,* edited by Richard H. Bube. *Westminster Theological Journal,* XXXI (May, 1969), 217-24.

———. Review of *Evolution and Christian Faith,* by Bolton Davidheiser. *Westminster Theological Journal,* XXXIII:2 (May, 1971), 222-24.

———. Review of *Symposium on Creation—II,* edited by

Donald W. Patten. *Westminster Theological Journal,* XXXIV:1 (November, 1971), 61-66.

Young, Edward J. *Studies in Genesis One.* Nutley, N.J.: Presbyterian and Reformed Pub. Co., 1964.

index
of names and subjects

index
of Scripture

38:39 — 76
40:15-19 — 28

Psalms
29:1-10 — 54
29:10 — 36, 48
33:7 — 38
36:9 — 144
104:6 — 54
104:6-9 — 35, 38
104:7-8 — 40
104:8 — 35, 39
104:9 — 36
119:18 — 107

Proverbs
8:22-31 — 38
22:13 — 76

Ecclesiastes
1:6 — 103

Isaiah
1:9 — 132
13:19 — 132
24:18 — 34
40:12 — 33
54:9 — 33, 35, 36, 38

Jeremiah
2:2 — 31
5:22 — 36, 38
20:16 — 132
31:20 — 20
33:20-25 — 103
49:18 — 132

Amos
1:1 — 103
4:11 — 132

Zephaniah
2:9 — 132

Zechariah
14:5 — 103

Malachi
3:10 — 34

Matthew
5:18 — 97
16:2-3 — 103
19:4 — 71, 96
21:16 — 96
22:29 — 18, 96, 107
24:37-42 — 17, 18
24:39 — 53, 71
27:57-66 — 129
28:2 — 129
28:18-20 — 59

Mark
7:7-8 — 42
10:15 — 141
12:15 — 96
16:4 — 129

Luke
1:54-55 — 31
16:31 — 51, 96
17:26-27 — 17, 53, 71
17:29-32 — 71, 132
23:43 — 32
24:25 — 96

John
5:46-47 — 96
8:31 — 130
12:48 — 96
20:1-13 — 129
20:19-26 — 129

Acts
1:3 — 120
2:5 — 61
14:17 — 9
17:11 — 107
18:24-25 — 10
26:26 — 120

Romans
1:4 — 122
5:12 — 28
8:20-22 — 28
10:9 — 18, 122, 130

I Corinthians
1:20 — 144

L.I.F.E. College Library
1100 Glendale Blvd.
Los Angeles, Calif. 90026